A TASTE OF

POWER

First printing September, 1973

Cover design by Isobel Randall and Danie van Zyl

ISBN 0 86975 025 9

The assistance of S.M. Printer's Consultants in producing this book is acknowledged
with thanks

Printed by Ravan Press (Pty.) Ltd.,
Pharmacy House, 80 Jorissen Street,
Braamfontein, Johannesburg.

305.8068

SPRO-CAS PUBLICATION NUMBER 11

A TASTE OF

POWER

The final, co-ordinated Spro-cas Report

by

PETER RANDALL

Director of Spro-cas

THE STUDY PROJECT ON CHRISTIANITY
IN APARTHEID SOCIETY

JOHANNESBURG   1973

CONTENTS

APPENDIX: SELECTED DOCUMENTS

Document

PART ONE

TOWARDS THE NEW SOCIETY

For the New Black, this is a preparatory stage. The means are not now available for entering the final road. Our task therefore is to prepare for ten, fifteen and forty years. The only question now is whether black people are made of such stuff as histories are made of, and black people must answer that question in the presence of the world and in the presence of the black living, the black dead and the black unborn.

Bennie A. Khoapa in B. S. Biko (ed):
Black Viewpoint, Spro-cas Black Community
Programmes, 1972.

We have to be unified by our common desire to take the initiative in deciding and determining our future and that of future generations of black South Africans. We have mutual knowledge of the ways in which we have been deprived of this right. In their temporal dimensions, black consciousness and solidarity must mean something more than sheer nostalgia. In their present and future thrusts, they must mean the birth of a new creativity.

N. Chabani Manganyi: *Being-black-
in-the-World*, Spro-cas Publications, 1973.

Chapter One

INTRODUCTION

THEMES AND DIRECTIONS

The first major theme of this report, as it must be with any report on contemporary South Africa, is that the South African social system is in urgent need of radical change, in the sense of a fundamental redistribution of power and resources. The aim must be to re-allocate power so that the black majority can exercise an effective role in the decision-making processes of the society and gain a more equitable share of the land's resources.

Among the important pre-conditions for the achievement of such change are the right of all the people to a share in effective political power; the right of all workers to participate in legally recognised trade unions; a significant redistribution of the land, of wealth, and of income; radical changes to the existing educational system, and the right of all the people to equal educational opportunity; and the right of all the people to effective social security benefits *(1)*.

Radical change in this direction is imperative not only because it is morally right that we should seek to create an equitable social order and to eliminate discrimination, injustice and inequality, but also because it is the only way in which we can hope to secure a stable and relatively peaceful future for all the people of this country.

Black Initiative

A second major theme is that the kind of fundamental change indicated above all will be initiated by blacks, and that the white oligarchy, which to now has exercised a virtual monopoly of political and economic power, will increasingly have to respond to black initiatives. We are in the early stages of a new historical phase in South Africa, in which the initiative for change is passing into black hands. The tempo of this process can only accelerate, no matter what temporary setbacks black initiative may receive and no matter what efforts are made to thwart it, so that it is possible to discern already the beginnings of a transference of power. Blacks have begun to have a taste of power, and whites are not going to be able indefinitely to prevent them enjoying the full meal *(2)*.

One symptom of the process is to be seen in the roles being played by homeland leaders like Chief Gatsha Buthelezi of KwaZulu and Paramount Chief

Kaiser Matanzima of the Transkei, who are increasingly being joined in their outspoken criticism of government policies and their demands for more land, more resources and more power by other homeland leaders like Prof. H. Ntsanwisi, Chief L. Mangope and Mr N.C. Phatudi. Calls for a summit meeting of homeland leaders to forge a common strategy based on black solidarity are frequently heard. The white central government is increasingly being thrown on to the defensive by the homeland leaders, finding that it must constantly respond to their initiatives.

Another symptom is the militant stance being adopted (despite government harassment) by SASO (the black South African Students' Organisation) and the Black Peoples' Convention (an overtly political movement aimed at black solidarity and rejecting the homeland system). The Labour Party (which won the majority of seats in the last elections for the Coloured Persons' Representative Council, but which is in opposition since the white government then packed the council with its own nominees) and the Natal Indian Congress (despite the banning of Mewa Ramgobin, one of the driving forces in the resuscitation of the body) have likewise adopted militant anti-government stances.

At a profoundly significant level there is the growing ability of black labour to organise itself and to press its demands in a militant and coherent manner, as expressed, for example, in the strikes in Natal, the Eastern Cape, Cape Town and the Witwatersrand during 1972 and early 1973, which followed the dramatic Ovambo strikes of 1971-1972.

All these processes must be seen in the context, not only of a response to immediate hardship and frustration, but of a sweeping growth of Black Consciousness that whites can no longer complacently dismiss as a phenomenon confined to the black 'intelligentsia'. Whites will ignore at their own peril the manifestations of Black Consciousness among students and workers, and the development of related concepts like Black Theology, Black Drama and Black Poetry. There is in fact a cultural and intellectual ferment in the black community which is at least as important, both culturally and in terms of socio-political significance, as anything emanating from the white community *(3)*.

There is a clear movement towards a new Black Solidarity based on Black Consciousness ('black' being understood here as all those who, not being classified 'white', experience oppression by whites). A recent dramatic manifestation of this growth of solidarity is to be seen in the gathering of 12 000 people at Athlone, a Coloured township near Cape Town, to demand the unconditional re-admission of all students to the University of the Western Cape after the University Council had closed the institution following student protests and had demanded new applications, thereby clearly aiming to eliminate the 'ring-leaders' of the 'agitation'. It is of considerable significance that that mass meeting, which may serve as a turning point in the history both of Black Solidarity and of Coloured-white relationships, was addressed by an African, Chief Buthelezi, and an Indian, Mrs Fatima Meer, as well as by Coloured leaders like Adam Small and Sonny Leon.

White Responses

It is important to consider the response of the white power structure in South Africa to this changing situation. The white power structure has been defined as 'the interlocking system of white-dominated institutions whose actions, directly and indirectly, determine the access to power and available opportunities, and the distribution of resources', and 'those institutions and structures created by white enterprise and management, white labour and white government which function so as to exclude blacks from exercising effective power' *(4)*. One significant example of this is the legislation passed by the white government, with the support of most white labour, to deny effective trade union rights to African workers. Even the recent 'concessions' allowing Africans to advance to the position of 'aide' on the gold mines came about through exclusively white bargaining between management, labour, and government.

Increasingly, however, the true symbol of the white power structure is the white parliament, where decisions are taken and laws are passed that affect the lives of all the people of the country, whether enfranchised or not, whether residents of homelands or of 'white' South Africa. The white parliament, with its *toenadering* between the major white parties, its searching after white consensus on the fundamental matters of race relations and security, is now *par excellence* the instrument of white solidarity and white supremacy, and of Afrikaner nationalist imperialism. Any initiatives for fundamental change from whites are increasingly going to come from extra-parliamentary forces. *Verligte Aksie* and Mr Gerdener's Action South and Southern Africa are only two fairly superficial illustrations of this. There is thus a growing polarisation between those whites who support the white government and the white parliament in its role of defender of the existing social order, and those who increasingly are coming to recognise that the initiative is passing into other hands.

Among the latter are a considerable section of English intellectual leaders in the Universities, the Churches and the press, who resent and reject also the element of Afrikaner nationalist imperialism and the attempt to impose unacceptable norms, not only in personal and group relations but also in such matters as censorship and personal morality.

So within the overall black-white polarisation it is also possible to discern a polarisation within the white community itself, between English and Afrikaner nationalist values, between authoritarian and liberal modes, between young and old, and between cultural values and life styles. The clash was starkly symbolised in June 1972 when short-haired Afrikaner policemen beat long-haired English students in the precincts of an Anglican Cathedral for protesting in public against the educational inequalities suffered by blacks.

The response of the white power structure (primarily symbolised by the white government) to initiatives for change has been clearly intransigent, as in the case of overt political action by blacks, where an attempt was made to crush SASO and the BPC through the banning of its leaders in March 1973, which can possibly be seen as a continuation of the actions against the ANC and the PAC in the sixties.

White opponents of the regime are also victims of this intransigence (bannings of NUSAS leaders, of churchmen like Fr Desmond, withdrawals of passports, and the whole motivation behind the Schlebusch Commission). As the forces of change grow in scope and strength so they evoke, and will increasingly evoke, counter-forces of repression and reaction (more bannings, more 'trials by commission', more 'security' legislation, increased use of the network of spies and informers and other facets of the 'security' apparatus, more threats against press freedom and other civil rights) *(5)*.

We are thus in a period in which the immediate future is likely to be marked by continued intolerance of dissent, whether by white or black, and increased hostility towards activity aimed at socio-political change. This will in turn accelerate the processes of polarisation and confrontation in the society, with all the dangers and challenges this entails, together with the opportunities it will provide for creative work for change.

This analysis must be balanced, however, by recognising that the response of the white power structure to black initiatives for change has been of a dual nature. (Paradoxically, white dissent is less likely to be tolerated than black, since it is ultimately weaker and since white dissenters cannot be allowed to subvert white solidarity). On the one hand, there is the intransigence, the attempt to stifle and destroy. Apart from the actions against SASO and the BPC, there have been the bannings of books like *Black Theology, Cry Rage* and *Creativity and Black Development*. Everything possible is done to present the black community as divided and fragmented and to oppose the development of Black Solidarity. The picture presented to readers of the Afrikaans press bears little relation to the reality. Thus, for example, Mr Tom Swartz, the government-appointed chairman of the Coloured Persons' Representative Council, is presented as the authentic voice of the Coloured people, who condemns 'Bantu interference' by Chief Buthelezi in the affairs of the University of the Western Cape, and who disputes Adam Small's assertions of Black Solidarity across the black ethnic lines *(6)*.

On the other hand, however, there are some accommodations to meet a changed reality. The government's capitulation to the Coloured students is one example. Another is the partial recognition, since the 1973 strikes, of the right of African workers to strike. This is particularly significant since the strikers had in fact acted in clear defiance of the law, and yet almost no attempt was made to prosecute them, partly on account of the very large numbers involved and partly because of the dangers that would have accompanied mass arrests. Another is the increased willingness of government spokesmen like Deputy Minister Janson to abandon the myth that urban Africans are temporary sojourners in 'white' urban areas, and a corresponding willingness to accept that they will be needed for all time to keep the wheels of industry turning and hence that more technical training must be provided for Africans in urban areas.

Meaningful Change

The crucial question about the future potential for a relatively peaceful resolution (varying degrees of conflict are inevitable) is the degree to which the white power structure will accommodate to the need for a fundamental sharing of wealth, land and power *(7)*. The short-term prospects are not auspicious, at least on the surface, as is evidenced, for example, by the out-of-hand rejections of patently justified demands by homeland leaders like Buthelezi and Matanzima for more land.

The 'accommodations' already noted, and others like 'multi-national sport' (a response to the growing isolation in sport of South Africa, and representing a distinct shift in government policy, no matter how much apologists may seek to deny this) and the use of blacks in positions previously reserved for whites, both in government under-takings like the Post Office and the Railways *(8)* and in the mining industry (responses to the lack of sufficient skilled white manpower), are essentially marginal changes which do not fundamentally affect the basic inequalities of the social system. The Spro-cas Economics Commission has described the process as follows: 'employment policies are constantly adjusted whereby greater use is made of black labour without a concomitant adjustment of the socio-economic structure towards a more just society' *(9)*.

When pragmatic adjustments like these are taken together with other encouraging signs in the white community like the emergence of *Verligte Aksie* (which represents a readiness by a significant body of Afrikaner businessmen, academics and intellectuals to re-think the political situation in the country, as well as a weakening of in-group nationalistic feeling *(10)*), there is sometimes a tendency to believe that significant change is in the offing, that the situation is very fluid. The warning of the Spro-cas Social Commission is relevant here:

These trends might indeed be significant — in fact some of them un-doubtedly are — but they cannot and should not be uncritically accepted as indications that the structure of white supremacy and racial in-equality is weakening. Facile speculation which takes yesterday's events as a standard for assessing the significance of today's news is dangerous. It engenders false optimism. It encourages the notion that press statements and public protests can tip the scales of political fort-une. This sensitivity to the superficial blinds many people to the lessons of past decades, during which the basic structure of inequality has persisted despite many marginal adjustments in political terminology and practice. White supremacy is no delicate plant which will wilt in a slightly changed political, social or economic climate.

Nor, however, is apartheid necessarily like an eternal oak which will grow ever more massive and tough until destroyed in the fire of revolut-ion. The basic patterns of inequality might be largely resistant to the effects of many of the issues enumerated, but there are potentially power-ful contradictions in these patterns, and these contradictions imply the probability of conflicts, not necessarily violent or revolutionary, which, in the long run, will change the pattern of our society *(11)*.

White opponents of the apartheid system, if they react only to the super-ficial events in our society, tend to alternate between cautious euphoria at the latest 'breakthrough' (for example, recognition of the right of African workers to strike, or a multi-racial sports team) and profound gloom at the latest act of intolerant repression (for example, the virtual outlawing of peace-ful protest). It is only by seeing the situation steadily and seeing it whole, by being aware of the historical roots of the present social patterns, and by re-cognising the powerful underlying social forces, that whites can keep some perspective and continue to recognise that change, major change, is, after all, inevitable.

Finally, the question must arise whether South Africa's 'traditional' economic structures are capable of enabling the kind of fundamental change defined at the beginning of this chapter, or whether we should be exploring far more vigorously the potential alternatives offered by socialist forms of society, including those which have been developed in other parts of Africa *(12)*.

Acknowledgment

In this Introduction I have tried, by rather baldly and dogmatically stating a series of assumptions and propositions, to provide a conceptual framework for this final Spro-cas report which must, in the nature of Spro-cas itself, deal primarily with the problems of social, economic and political change in South Africa.

While I must bear full responsibility for what is written in this report, at the same time I must acknowledge my deep indebtedness to the six Spro-cas study commissions in whose work I have participated for four years and on whose conclusions and findings I have drawn very heavily, merely attempting to update these with new information where this has seemed necessary. My own political and intellectual development owes a very great deal to these commissions and to those I have worked with in Spro-cas 2, and I am deeply privileged to have shared with so many fine minds in a probing analysis of the situation in our country and in the search for a changed social and political order.

FOOTNOTES

1. See *Power, Privilege and Poverty*, report of the Spro-cas Economics Commission (1972), p. 103-104.
2. It is interesting to see that some perceptive Afrikaners are recognising the validity of this analysis. Mr Lieb Loots, a former SRC President of the Rand Afrikaans University, speaking at the inaugural congress of *Verligte Aksie* in June 1973, warned that 'the black man had taken over political initiative from the Afrikaner, and *verligtes* had to find out how to react to black initiative' (Report to 50th NUSAS Congress by Geoff Budlender). Similarly, Prof. S.P. Cilliers, head of the department of Sociology at Stellenbosch University, has been quoted as saying that he had gained the impression that blacks had seized the political initiative from whites (*Rand Daily Mail*, 9 July 1973). And Dr J.S. Kruger, senior lecturer in dogma, ethics and practical theology at the University of South Africa, has said that the Afrikaans Churches 'should accept that the blacks would gain power in South Africa and it was only good and proper that the power monopoly of the white man should be broken' (*Rand Daily Mail*, 12 July 1973).
3. See, for example, *Black Review 1972* (Black Community Programmes) pp 201 ff; N.C. Manganyi: *Being-black-in-the-World* (Spro-cas, 1973); Nadine Gordimer: *The Black Interpreters* (Spro-cas, 1973). Other examples are the three major African dramatic presentations during the Aquarius Arts Festival at the University of the Witwatersrand in June 1973; the poetry of James Matthews and Gladys Thomas (*Cry Rage*, published by Spro-cas 1972), Wally Serote (*Yakal 'NKomo*, published by Rhenoster Books 1973), Oswald Mtshali (*Sounds of a Cowhide Drum*, Rhenoster 1972) and others; *Black Theology*, published by the University Christian Movement, and the call for a Black Mission to Whites by Dr Manas Buthelezi and others (see *Pro Veritate*, June 1973); and *Creativity and Black Development*, published by SASO in 1973. (This is by no means an exhaustive list).
4. *Power, Privilege and Poverty*, op. cit., p. 33.
5. One recent indication of this is the decision to prosecute 47 people who took part in a silent protest on the steps of St George's Cathedral, Cape Town, on 15 May 1973, against the Gatherings and Demonstrations Bill which was before parliament at the time. Particularly indicative of disregard for a large sector of public opinion is the fact that those charged include leaders of the Labour Party, the Progressive Party, the Black Sash, NUSAS, the Civil Rights League, the SRC of the University of Cape Town, academics, clergy, and a Cape Town city councillor (*Cape Times*, 5 July 1973). (Charges were subsequently withdrawn).

6.   'Tom Swart verdoem Bantoe-inmenging', *Die Vaderland*, 10 July 1973.
7.   For a realistic assessment of possible accommodations see *South Africa's Political Alternatives*, report of the Spro-cas Political Commission, Chapter 13.
8.   See *Power, Privilege and Poverty*, op. cit., p. 91.
9.   Ibid., p. 67.
10.   *Towards Social Change*, report of the Spro-cas Social Commission, p. 157.
11.   Ibid., p. 158.
12.   This is, of course, a threatening exercise for the white government and it was perhaps inevitable that the author of the one recent effort in this direction has been banned: R. Turner: *The Eye of the Needle* (Spro-cas, 1972).

The important thing to remember about apartheid, segregation or what you will, is that it is designed to keep the black man as cheap labour to serve the white man's needs while ensuring that all wealth, prestige symbols and political power are effectively held in the white man's own capable hands. All other arguments, like 'development along their own lines', 'separate development' etc., are just so much eyewash for a policy that has nothing to commend it but the rapacity of the white man

Nimrod Mkele: *Domesticating the African*,
unpublished paper, 1959.

Chapter Two

APARTHEID SOCIETY

THE SOCIAL STRUCTURES

The urgent need for change in the apartheid society has been demonstrated frequently and since even before Nimrod Mkele was writing in 1959. Since then, of course, there has been Sharpeville, the establishment of the Republic, the outlawing of the African National Congress and the Pan-Africanist Congress, the movement towards the creation of political sub-systems for black South Africans, the extension and entrenchment of migrant labour, the spread of Black Consciousness, the Rhodesian UDI, the escalation of guerilla warfare in Southern Africa, the ending of multi-racial political activity, the intensification of foreign pressures on the South African political and economic systems, the growing military preparedness of the South African regime, and the growing dangers of massive racial confrontation in the subcontinent. It is morally unacceptable, socially unhealthy and politically dangerous that there should be grave poverty and powerlessness juxtaposed with great wealth and power in the same society. In South Africa we have a picture of white comfort, white privilege and white power. The diseases of white people are often those of affluence and over-eating, the diseases of black people are often those of poverty and malnutrition. It is the monopoly of political power in the hands of whites and their disproportionate share of the country's wealth that has led to a gross imbalance between the race groups, and makes South Africa a microcosm of the world problem of rich whites and poor blacks.

In the words of the Spro-cas Economics Report: 'where there is great poverty, an enormous gap between rich and poor is obscene. One mark of the Responsible Society is surely that it will be structured to eliminate as far as possible poverty, hunger, and damp, overcrowded housing. The provision of a social security net below which the helpless and the weak may not be allowed to fall should be top priority for any true development' *(1)*.

The Basic Patterns

Every institution in our society reflects the basic patterns of enforced racial segregation, discrimination in favour of whites, inequality in the provision of resources and facilities, and inequality of opportunity. From birth to death we live in a segregated, discriminatory, unequal and unjust society. Black babies

GOD REST YE MERRY, GENTLEMEN

This Spro-cas poster, designed by Franco Frescura, conveys starkly an essential message of the Spro-cas Economics Report. It is interesting that the poster has evoked far more vehement responses from whites than the report. One white clergyman ordered that it should be removed from his church notice board because it was 'shocking, racist and non-Christian'.

die more often than white ones *(2)*: infant mortality rates are highest for Africans and lowest for whites, with Coloured and Indian in between. It has been authoritatively estimated that at least half of all babies in a typical African homeland die before their fifth birthdays *(3)*.

Reproduced from the magazine of the Vrije Universiteit, Amsterdam, this Spro-cas poster sought to startle whites into an awareness of their own avarice and materialism. The Afrikaner nationalist party-organ, *Die Vaderland,* described it as 'shocking', a 'smear', and 'highly irresponsible'. The same paper completely ignored the reports of the Spro-cas study commissions, although review copies were regularly sent to it.

EDUCATION

Education is free and compulsory for whites, but not for blacks. The state spends approximately fifteen times as much on each white schoolchild as it does on each African one, again with Coloured and Indian in between these extremes *(4)*. Coming from already disadvantaged home backgrounds, black children have nothing like the well-developed pre-school system available to whites. They face additional financial burdens compared to whites, since they must generally purchase their own books and stationery and pay school levies, if they are fortunate enough to be admitted to a school. Their teachers, who often have to teach double sessions, are generally poorly qualified and poorly paid, and their classes are three times as large, on average, as those of whites.

No wonder there is a high drop-out rate, with fully one quarter of African children leaving school after their first year, and less than one per cent proceeding to the end of the secondary school. By the end of Standard 2 more than half the African children admitted in Sub-A will have left to join the street gangs, the newspaper vendors, the glue-sniffers and the crowds of caddies who are sometimes controlled with whips and dogs as they clamour for work. Their so-called education has been virtually useless, almost a total waste of time and money, since they are not even literate in an African language, their white masters having decided that on top of all their other disadvantages they should start learning English and Afrikaans, as well as their vernacular, during their first year at school. According to the Spro-cas Education Commission this would seem to be a linguistic burden unique in the history of formal education, and one motivated by nothing more noble than a self-defeating wish to impose, and thereby entrench, the Afrikaans language. As the homelands have acquired increased control over their education departments, it has been inevitable that they should reject many of the basic policies of 'Bantu Education', including the policy regarding media of instruction. It is clear that in time the homelands will all adopt English as the medium from the end of the lower primary school.

When they have finally reached the maxima of their salary scales, an African teacher, an Indian head of a division in a technical college, and a Coloured lecturer at the University of the Western Cape still earn less than the starting salaries of their white colleagues with the same qualifications *(5)*, even though they are all absorbed in the common South African economy, and all have to pay prevailing market prices.

This has been an attempt to provide a brief overview of the education system, which must, like the other basic social institutions, be expected to reflect the patterns of discrimination and inequality of the broader society. It is not a complete and exhaustive picture since the Spro-cas Education Commission has already made a comprehensive analysis of unacceptable principles and unacceptable practices in South African education (6).

Recent data has borne out the findings of the Commission. For example, the 1972 Report of the Tswana homeland (Bophuthatswana) Department of Education, now partially under the control of the homeland authority, reveals a depressing picture of unqualified teachers (25 per cent of the total teaching force), a lack of classroom accommodation (more than 3 000 class-rooms are needed), overcrowded classes (sometimes 90 pupils in a room), double sessions and a high drop-out rate (55,4 per cent of the pupils in Stand-ard 6 dropped out, many because of insufficient school accommodation) (7). It is probable that the picture is substantially the same in the other homelands.

The developments that have occurred in the education system since the Spro-cas Report was published in August 1971 reflect both gains and losses. A significant shift in government policy, in line with a major recommendation of the Commission, was the decision to abolish the Bantu Education Account and to finance 'Bantu Education' directly from General Revenue. The State has consequently been able to make more money available for African schools (although a rise in per capita expenditure from R20 to R25 should be seen against a rise from R197 to R223 per capita for white pupils in the Trans-vaal in a single year (8)). In line with most 'social change' in South Africa in the past two years, this implies that while the position of blacks may have improved marginally in absolute terms, the relative advantage enjoyed by whites has improved yet further. The gap has widened, rather than narrowed.

Government policy has shifted also in accordance with a greater willing-ness to recognise that blacks will always remain in the urban areas and that the continued economic prosperity of the whole society, including the whites, depends on a sufficient supply of trained and skilled labour. There is a suggestion that government leaders may in fact be increasingly prepared to accept the embourgeoisment of urban blacks as a strategy, in line with the old liberal argument that a 'contented middle class' is the best bulwark against Communist and other agitation. Hence a greater willingness to erect second-ary schools and technical and commercial colleges in black urban townships, and to encourage schemes like TEACH (Teach Every African Child), run by the Johannesburg *Star*, which has had phenomenal success in raising funds to build classrooms and in fact whole schools in Soweto (the total collected by July 1973 was R500 000, which has been used to build 20 schools). Cynics of course will see in this also a willingness by the State to allow the public to shoulder some of the financial responsibility which should rest on the State alone.

Laudable as TEACH (and similar schemes like LEARN) may be, two possible dangers should be borne in mind: support by whites might be merely a conscience-salving gesture, leaving them persuaded that no further action is required, and it might increase black dependency on white charity, thus sapping initiative.

While there has been much talk of the need for compulsory education for blacks in the past year, no visible progress has been made in this direction for Africans, although there has been some progress regarding Coloured and Indian education. The rectors of the (white) Afrikaans universities issued a statement after the student protests of June 1972, which were aimed at bringing about an awareness of the need for free and compulsory education for all South Africans, in which they condemned such a call as 'totally unrealistic'. This language was stronger than that used by the Cape Superintendent-General of Education in 1920, who called universal compulsory education at that juncture 'desirable but not practicable' *(9)*.

After defending racially segregated education, the Afrikaans rectors concluded that the student protests were aimed at a 'radical revolution of the social and political order in our country' which they and their universities 'will oppose with all our might' *(10)*. Similar attitudes were evinced by the Broad Moderature of the largest Afrikaans Church, the Nederduits Gereformeerde Kerk ('control this permissiveness and these carefully planned methods of creating chaos and destroying peace and order') and by Dr A.L. Kotzee, the Director of Education in the Transvaal ('student unrest on the campus is being planned internally by communist and nihilist groups — their aim is anarchy and the destruction of Western civilisation, piece by piece') *(11)*.

These views clearly accord with the mounting intolerance of any forms of protest and dissent by whites already mentioned in Chapter One, and are in line with recent government actions like the bannings of NUSAS and SASO leaders, the setting up of the Schlebusch Commission, and the Gatherings and Demonstrations Act. The response to such intransigence has been a hardening of attitude by both the small group of white radicals and the large body of black students, seen, for example, in refusals to co-operate with the Schlebusch Commission on the one hand, and on the other hand, boycotts and other protests in July 1973 on black campuses like the University of the Western Cape and the Rand College of Education, and the increased militancy of SASO's attitude towards whites generally *(12)*.

The polarising conflict has been described as follows: 'The advent of Youth Preparedness, with its military component for both (white) sexes, is ominous .... symptomatic of an intolerance which is moving in the direction of 'shut up or we'll bash you up', which is the hallmark of 'right-thinking' totalitarian youth movements .... Add to this the clearly growing militancy of black youth, and we have a recipe for violent conflict which educators seem powerless to stop ....' *(13)*.

This Spro-cas poster, designed by Rob Collins, was issued during the student protests of June 1972. The Afrikaans nationalist party-organ, *Die Transvaler*, described it in an editorial as 'a scandalous Hitler-poster which tries to brand the government' (*Die Transvaler*, 7 July 1973). Like its stablemate, *Die Vaderland*, this paper has virtually ignored the serious studies of the Spro-cas Commissions.

THE ECONOMY

White per capita incomes — now amongst the highest in the world *(14)* — are on average more than thirteen times as high as African incomes *(15)*. The House of Commons Sub-Committee enquiring into British employment practices in South Africa heard evidence that African labourers at mines controlled by a British group were paid as little R3 a week *(16)*. At the other end of the scale, advertisements for 'top executives' (white) frequently appear in the South African press offering salaries of R25 000 or more.

The patterns of poverty and the lack of social security experienced by the bulk of black South Africans have been fully documented in the reports of the Spro-cas Economics and Social Commissions, and so will not be repeated here. A striking example of the built-in racial discrimination in the country's economic system is, however, provided by the tax system, which those commissions did not analyse fully.

Despite discrepancies in income, which already discriminate grossly in favour of whites, blacks have to bear additional tax burdens *(17)*. All Africans, whatever their age or the size of their families, begin paying income tax when their incomes reach R360 a year. Other racial groups begin paying only at R676 a year, and if they are married they start at R1151 a year; if they have one child at R1601; if they have three children at R2601. In addition, all African men over 18 pay a fixed general tax of R2,50 a year (the 'poll tax', a relic of the days when Africans were taxed to persuade them to work for whites) whether they are earning or not. Failure to produce proof of payment (a stamp in his pass book) renders an African liable to arrest without a warrant. More than 105 000 Africans were in fact prosecuted for 'Bantu' tax infringements between July 1970 and June 1971. (It goes without saying that this is also an effective mechanism for controlling the movement of Africans). White widows are regarded as married for tax purposes and their tax liability is reduced accordingly; African widows pay at the rate applicable to a single person. Whites over 60 have tax abatements, Africans do not. There are other anomalies, but perhaps enough has been said to substantiate the view that the tax system discriminates against blacks.

It is indicative of the extent of black poverty that, despite such extraordinary measures to squeeze taxes from Africans, the total yielded from African income tax in 1970-71 was only R6,8 million, while the 'poll tax' produced R8,1 million *(18)*. Clearly a removal of the discrimination would mean a very small loss to the State, which in any case receives a very substantial contribution to the Exchequer through indirect taxes paid by Africans.

The discriminatory tax system is merely symptomatic of the discriminatory nature of the economic system as a whole. White trade unions are legally recognised, black ones are not. The bargaining position of black workers is further weakened by 'considerable harrassment of leaders who, by means of banning orders etc., have been removed from positions from which they were stimulating the growth of the black trade union movement' *(19)*. The virtual exclusion of African workers from the decision-making processes of the main wage regulating mechanisms, the Industrial Councils and the Wage Board, and the extent to which this represents 'institutionalised violence' have been analysed in the Spro-cas Economics Report *(20)*. All these factors contribute to the power of the white worker in maintaining his privileged position, and to the powerlessness of the black worker in seeking to improve his.

In a country whose government prides itself on its firm commitment to the principles of free enterprise, it is paradoxical that access to entrepreneurial opportunity is heavily limited for the bulk of the people. As a result of various restrictive and discriminatory measures, black entrepreneurs probably have less freedom of entrepreneurial action than foreign investors *(21)*. White entrepreneurs have much greater freedom to pursue profits, even in African townships like Soweto, thus making a mockery of the high-sounding principles of separate development.

Large categories of black workers are excluded from the provisions of the Unemployment Insurance Act. The benefits from the Workmen's Compensation Fund are sometimes used for whites only, although the levy is the same for employees of all races. Old age pensions paid by the State reveal the usual discriminatory norms: white pensions are double those of Coloureds and Indians and seven times those of Africans *(22)*.

The 'single most important distinguishing feature of the South African economy' is how the Spro-cas Economics Commission describes migrant labour. It can be regarded as the cornerstone of the economy and, in the words of the Commission, is 'fundamentally evil in its operation' *(23)*. The 'vast changes that have been taking place in the structure of the black labour force since the mid-1960's' *(24)* are primarily the result of the increased implementation of the migrant labour system. The government stated in 1968 its intention of building the country's economy on migrant labour. The destruction of settled communities, with single-sex hostels replacing family homes, as in Alexandra Township near Johannesburg, is but one step in the process. There are about 1 500 000 migrant workers in South Africa and Namibia; when their families are taken into account, the system probably affects six million people.

Comprehensive documentation exists on the evils of migrant labour, and Dr Francis Wilson's monumental study has detailed its extent as well as giving constructive proposals for phasing it out. The relationship between migrant labour and other aspects of economic and social life in South Africa has been vividly described by John Kane-Berman in a Spro-cas Background Paper *(25)*:

The main instrument for enforcing the migratory labour system is the pass laws. Nearly 1 800 people are prosecuted every day of the year for technical offences under the pass laws. Africans in the townships live in terror of police raids — at night and with dogs. Arrest can mean the loss of a job, prison, and ultimately deportation to some remote and poverty-stricken rural area where there may be no jobs and no houses.

The human costs of the system are enormous. Migrants usually have to live in barrack-like single-sex hostels or compounds. Wives cannot live with their husbands, nor parents with their children. The inevitable results are prostitution (both male and female), adultery, illegitimacy, venereal diseases, juvenile delinquency, drunkenness. Numerous studies have shown time and again that these social evils are rife in South Africa.

The system also helps to perpetuate poverty. Workers shuttling back and forth between town and country do not stay long enough in any one job to acquire much more than rudimentary skills. Industry does not consider it worthwhile to train workers beyond a certain level if these workers have to leave the company to return to the rural areas before the increased productivity arising from their training has compensated the company for providing that training. In other words, the migratory labour system discourages the economy from investing in its labour force. This lack of industrial training is a major cause of poverty — poverty which brings misery and violence and crime in its wake.

Migratory labour involves a vicious circle. The work-force is unstable and ill-trained and wages are low. The reserves get poorer as the population increases. More Africans thus have to leave to find work in the towns. Because they have to export their male manpower the reserves get even poorer still. Meanwhile industries expand and the whites get richer, but black wages remain low because of the large supply of cheap labour.

Consolidation schemes for the homelands, 'black spot' removals and 'closer settlement' schemes in the homelands all play their part in extending and perpetuating migrant labour. A recent article on the Basotho Qwa Qwa homeland, centred on Witsieshoek, has described how part of the process operates *(26)*. Since the establishment of the homeland's Legislative Assembly in 1972, South Sotho people have been moving to Witsieshoek at the rate of 300 each month. Many of them have been forced to move in terms of government policy of clearing all 'superfluous Bantu' from the towns and villages of the Orange Free State. Others have moved voluntarily from white farms: the reason is that as farm labourers neither they nor their children can ever work as anything else, but as homeland residents they can sign up as contract workers in industry or mines in the OFS or the Witwatersrand. Since farm workers can earn as little as R5 a month *(27)*, even the R25 or R30 of a migrant worker must seem munificent in comparison. The sacrifice for the increased earnings is, of course, felt by the family, from whom the migrant is separated for periods of six months or a year.

Despite widespread concern about black wages during the first half of 1973, the general level remains very low, particularly in the mining industry, where the lowest income group still earns less than R24 per month *(28)*. Despite a 26 per cent rise for the Anglo-American Corporation's 120 000 African gold miners, their average monthly wage is still only R32 per month *(29)* (and at least 80 per cent of these men work underground). The rise must be seen in the context of a rise in the cost-of-living of nine per cent, and a rise in food prices of more than 14 per cent *(30)*. The *Financial Mail* concludes from these figures that the black miner's family in the homeland is likely to be starving. This is borne out by a survey conducted by the Anglo-American Corporation, which revealed that the average African gold-miner sends home twenty-eight per cent of his income. For many families this means less than R8 per month *(31)*.

The increases granted to black miners totalled R9,5 million. In 1972, the company's pre-tax gold-mining profits rose by about R80 million (or 50 per cent) to R238 million, which is nearly five times its total black wage bill. Even after-tax profits rose by 40 per cent to R140 million *(32)*. The *Financial Mail* concludes that the company could easily afford to double its African wages. The same can probably be said of all the large mining companies, particularly in the light of the tremendous increase in the world gold price during 1973. The figures for African miners must also be seen in the context of the additional R100 per month granted to white miners in June, 1973, which has effectively widened the income gap yet further. The 7 000 white artisans on the gold mines also received improved fringe benefits. A white journeyman can now earn R450 per month without overtime *(33)*.

As was the case with per capita expenditure in education, we have again an indicator that recent changes, while marginally improving the position of blacks in absolute terms, have actually left them further disadvantaged vis-a-vis whites.

It is significant that the bargaining which resulted in the improvements for both black and white miners was an exclusively white affair, with the Chamber of Mines on the one hand and the Federation of Mining Unions, representing five white artisan unions, on the other. In return for their extensive financial benefits, the white unions agreed to allow the advancement of Africans to the position of artisan 'aides' who will be permitted to do some of an artisan's tasks, at the discretion of the white artisan himself. About 12 000 to 14 000 Africans are likely to be affected by this scheme, less than four per cent of the goldmines' total African labour force *(34)*.

Advertisements that appeared in the *Sunday Times,* 2 September, 1973

This example illustrates yet again that only marginal changes are possible given the 'white monopolisation of power' through the white-controlled organisational and institutional network that, in the view of the Spro-cas Economics Commission, is 'the root cause of our irresponsible society'. The Commission concludes that 'real change will occur only when blacks are enabled to organise — through either trade unions or other quasi-political bodies — and exercise some bargaining power' *(35)*.

White control of the Wage Board machinery, which is the wage-regulating system for those industries not covered by Industrial Councils, reveals the same situation. Despite signs that the government had begun to realise the urgent need for a drastic raising of black wages following on the strikes at the beginning of 1973, the Wage Board proposals regarding unskilled wages reveal that 'in no instance will the proposed minima for adult males reach these (poverty datum) levels even at the end of the two-year spread' *(36)*. The proposals range from R10 per week, rising over two years to R12, for a male unskilled worker in East London (against a Poverty Datum Line, calculated by Prof. J.F. Potgieter of the University of Port Elizabeth, of R17,68) to R14,50, rising to R16,50, in 'certain Cape areas' (against a PDL of R18,88 *(37)*).

A movement in the right direction is, however, indicated by the growing recognition that cost-of-living rises should be taken into account in determining earnings. This is in line with the second recommendation for 'Immediate Steps' of the Spro-cas Economics Commission. For example, the Minister of Labour is reported to have ordered an immediate 25 per cent increase in the minimum wages paid to black building workers undertaking skilled work in African areas (which are the only areas where they may perform such work in terms of the Bantu Building Workers' Act) with provision for increases as the COL index rises *(38)*. This is again an illuminating example of the mixture of economic, ideological and political elements in the employment practices of the country. One can analyse the various components as:

(i)   a recognition that African workers, like other workers, need to be helped to withstand COL rises;

(ii)   a recognition that basic wages for black workers must be increased (this makes economic sense to white entrepreneurs, who wish to see the local consumer market expanded);

(iii) a recognition that there are insufficient white skilled workers;

(iv)   a fear of black skilled workers competing with whites, hence their restriction to the homelands;

(v)   a fear of the political reactions of white workers and their unions if blacks are allowed to perform skilled work in 'white' areas;

(vi)   a desire to develop the homelands thereby making them more attractive to blacks, thereby potentially reducing the number of blacks in 'white' areas;

(vii) and the whole decision-making process in the hands of a white Minister of Labour.

The Spro-cas Social Commission felt that there is a basic consensus amongst all the white groups to maintain white domination and hence white power and privilege. This was neatly illustrated as this report was being written when the Young Progressives, who should be the most 'radical' grouping within the formal white political system, rejected a resolution asking all employers to 'move towards' the payment of black wages above the 'effective minimum level' *(39)* (i.e. a level at which minimum standards of health and decency can be maintained). The reasons given, that (white) businessmen might become bankrupt, thus reducing employment opportunities for blacks, and that it was anyway up to the government to set the example in a capitalist country, were clearly rationalisations masking a fear of rocking the (white) boat.

THE LEGAL SYSTEM

The law itself sometimes embodies discrimination against people on account of their race. An especially significant example of this is the Bantu (Prohibition of Interdicts) Act of 1956, as amended by Act No 42 of 1964. This Act provides that if any African is required by an order to vacate any area or to be arrested or detained for the purpose of his removal therefrom, no interdict or other legal process may be obtained to stay or suspend the execution of the order. The effect of this is that if an African is ordered to leave any area (in terms of the Bantu Trust and Land Act or the Bantu Urban Areas Consolidation Act) he must obey the order and cannot invoke the protection of the Courts *(40)*.

The by-passing of the Courts by the legislature and the executive, and the consequent weakening of the safeguards of the citizen, are characteristics of the apartheid society. A significant example of this is provided by the decision of parliament to establish a commission of parliamentarians to investigate four organisations (the Schlebusch Commission), on the strength of whose findings (based on secret hearings at which those investigated had no legal rights) people have had their normal rights savagely restricted by the Minister of Justice. The Courts did not feature in the process at all. 'Law and Order' are deemed far more important than law and justice. An eminent Afrikaner academic, Prof S.A. Strauss, of the Law Faculty of the University of South Africa, has described the greatest threat to the basic values of South Africa's legal system as the kind of 'extra-judicial criminal law' which the

Suppression of Communism Act makes possible. Pointing out that the Act is employed against people who are not Communists, Prof Strauss concludes that 'we have thereby virtually abandoned the principle of legality' *(41)*.

The Spro-cas Political Commission *(42)* found that the real issue in the relationship between law and justice in South Africa is not the supposed antithesis between order and freedom: 'it is the real conflict between supporting the existing social structure and ideas and actions that strive to change it'. The real aim of much security legislation and action is 'to shore up the existing unequal order and to frustrate the evolution of a more just order'. The Commission believes that 'the rhetoric and the actions aimed at the goal of self-preservation are having catastrophic effects on white society, breeding values that are the antithesis of love, compassion and humanity'. It warns 'in the strongest terms that the growth of a militarist spirit is a serious cancer which, if unchecked, will nullify any claims which white South Africans may have to being custodians of the Judaeo-Christian tradition'.

One of the major conclusions in this section of the Report is that 'order of a kind and of a questionable permanence has indeed been maintained in our society, but it has extracted a high toll in terms of freedom. Over wide areas civil liberties have been eclipsed and the Rule of Law put in abeyance. The Security Police and the Bureau for State Security operate with what appears to outsiders as an infinite scope. Informers are believed to be at work in every corner of society; it is widely believed that telephones are tapped and that mail is interfered with. All these activities create a widespread fear in our society that these security agencies are steadily becoming a law unto themselves'.

It is well known that the dictum of 'separate but equal' does not apply in the South African legal system *(43)*, and the white parliament has passed legislation sanctioning the provision of unequal and inferior facilities for blacks. The law in fact sometimes compels the courts to treat people differently on account of their race *(44)*. The implementation of much legislation clearly works in favour of whites, as for example in removals under the Group Areas Act *(45)*.

In 1959, Nimrod Mkele asked: 'Is it surprising that the African shows little respect for the law when he sees before him such patent evidence of discrimination? In fact the surprising thing is that there are still so many law-abiding Africans when all Africans live as they do on the fringes of legality' *(46)*. Whereas in other plural societies, such as the USA, the laws protect those working for social change, and the intention of the law is usually to promote racial equality and justice, in South Africa the laws are more often used for the opposite purposes.

Apartheid legislation, the legal profession and the courts, the role of the police in the apartheid society, and the control and functioning of administr tiv odies such as the Group Areas Board and local Road Transportation

Boards are dealt with in the report of the Spro-cas Legal Commission. Mr Colin Kinghorn points out that 'the system of apartheid, as a 'colossal social experiment', is implemented very largely through administrative bodies' (which are controlled by whites, predominantly Afrikaner nationalist whites) and that where the courts have intervened between administrative bodies and individual citizens 'to prevent unreasonableness, discrimination and inequality of treatment, or to insist that the principles of natural justice be observed, the legislature has subsequently intervened to authorise unreasonableness, discrimination and inequality of treatment and expressly or impliedly to authorise departures from the principles of natural justice' *(47).*

It is at this level that the legal system particularly reflects the patterns of the broader society, and becomes an instrument in the maintenance of white power and privilege.

NOTE: Spro-cas Background Paper 5: Rule by Police or Rule by Law? by John Kane-Berman provides a useful summary of arbitrary action taken by the State against individuals in South Africa.

THE POLITICAL SYSTEM

South Africa's political system is a racial oligarchy in which all significant political power is vested in white hands. The Spro-cas Political Commission has analysed the erosion of black rights since the time of Union in 1910, to the point where the Republican parliament is now representative of white political interests only *(48).* This parliament is still the fount of power in South Africa and will continue to be however much power is devolved to separate political institutions created under the apartheid policy as presently envisaged.

It follows from this that inequality and injustice are built into the existing political system. The history of the franchise in South Africa shows a sustained, progressively exacerbated breach of the principle that all adults are entitled to effective political participation. From a limited measure of influence in the central political system, black participation has now been eliminated. 'Instead of the previous small amount of substance they are now offered shadow votes in bodies' (the homelands governments, the Coloured Persons' Representative Council, the South African Indian Council) 'which are incapable of satisfying their legitimate political aspirations' *(49).*

The conclusion of the Commission is significant: 'We wish to make it clear that we are not laying the blame for this injustice exclusively at the door of any one political party: the erosion of black political rights stems from processes that are inherent in the social system that has developed in South Africa' *(50).*

Clearly the most significant of these processes is the development of a broad white consensus on the need for political domination and economic privilege, but before looking more closely at the implications of this, we can briefly survey some current political developments. The Spro-cas Political Report has only recently appeared and includes developments in the first half of 1973, so that this survey need only be very brief and incomplete.

Some current developments have already been indicated in this report:

(i)   the growing impatience of homeland leaders and the repeated calls for a summit meeting to forge a common strategy;
(ii)   the growing militancy of black students and their ability to secure the support of their community;
(iii) the movement of the whole white political structure towards consensus on security and 'law and order';
(iv)   the increasingly totalitarian response of the State to internal dissent;
(v)   the growing guerilla threat to South Africa's white-ruled neighbours;
(vi)   increased foreign pressure on the Republic;
(vii) the growing militancy and bargaining ability of black workers;
(viii) the marginal accommodations being made in the socio-economic system to meet some of the developing forces.

We are experiencing a period of polarisation which must inevitably result in confrontations and crises. As this is being written the confrontation between the students and the authorities of the University of the Western Cape is continuing. Amongst other matters the students, backed by their community, are demanding an impartial enquiry into their grievances and that the white Afrikaner Rector of the University, Prof C.J. Kriel, should resign *(51)*. The political undertones are clear, particularly since the Rector and the University Council are government-appointed, and the final decisions lie with the Minister of 'Coloured Relations'. The students displayed considerable acumen and organising ability in holding meetings in the community around the country, putting their point of view and gaining the support of their parents and community leaders. The successful mass meeting of 12 000 in Athlone Township, addressed by Chief Buthelezi, Mrs Meer and Coloured leaders, and where, significantly enough, the SASO President was prepared to share the platform with a homeland leader, has already been mentioned. A perceptive columnist has described this meeting as of considerable political significance, suggesting that the attitudes of Coloured people are undergoing change and that black groups previously divided on grounds of ideology and strategy 'have decided to sink their differences to establish a common front' *(52)*.

In the same week protests erupted amongst Coloured students of the Rand College of Education, who boycotted lectures and submitted a memorandum listing their demands to the acting rector, Dr P. W. Bingle *(53)*. It is, of course, too early to assess the long-term implications of these events, but they cannot lightly be dismissed, as the authorities are fond of doing, as the work of a few 'agitators'.

Another confrontation is also building up around the Coloured Persons' Representative Council. The leader of the opposition Labour Party, Mr Sonny Leon, believes that Coloured people are foresaking their old pro-white allegiances and backing black consciousness and black solidarity *(54)*. Mr Leon pinpoints the problem as follows:

> Every year we make recommendations to the government, and every year they're turned down. Some minor concessions have been granted. And they've increased our Budget, which they control. But one of the cruellest ironies is that more and more white administrative staff are employed to run the CRC, and their salary bill is far higher than the salary bill of all CRC members, including the executive, put together.

An echo of this is heard in the complaint of a homeland leader, Chief Lucas Mangope of Bophutatswana, who finds it frustrating that his government is subservient to the Republican government: 'we can decide to send teachers abroad to become specialised in certain fields of education, but we do not have the right to issue them passports' *(55)*. The Republican government must inevitably become victim of a crisis of credibility among many of its own followers unless it soon more effectively devolves real power to the political sub-systems it has created as a rationalisation for the total exclusion of blacks from the central political system.

Another confrontation is building up over the question of the right of the Transkei government to appoint an African, Dr Charles Bikitsha, as medical superintendent of the Butterworth State Hospital. The Transkeian government and the Republic's Department of Health are in a state of deadlock over the appointment as this is being written, since it is the policy of the South African government that blacks should not be appointed in positions of authority over whites.

Realignments and re-groupings are beginning to occur to a significant degree, in response to the intransigence of white power and the refusal of the Republican government to make meaningful accommodations on basic issues which at present it regards as non-bargainable, in contrast to marginal issues which do not threaten white domination.

In Namibia, for example, all but one of the black opposition groups have formed a National Convention, having reached consensus 'despite South African taunts that the peoples and parties of SWA were incurably divided' *(56)*. Among the aims of the National Convention are: to fight for the total and complete freedom and independence of the population of Namibia; to eliminate group, tribal and racial identity based on colour and economic station; to eliminate racial oppression and economic exploitation. Membership is not open to members of 'the oppressive group or body'. A significant straw in the wind is the call for 'proposals on how the economy can be used for the benefit of everyone in the country'.

Another example from Namibia is the movement towards closer union of both the black and the white Lutheran Churches, the political consequences of which are potentially very great. A united Lutheran Church would cut right across the South African government's policy of 'multi-national', 'multi-ethnic' development. Ironically enough, the catalyst for the movement was the government's action in arbitrarily expelling a German Lutheran pastor, Wolfgang Kruger, from Namibia *(57)*.

The co-operation between the KwaZulu government and trade union leaders in Natal in setting up an institute for the training of black workers in trade unionism is another interesting illustration of current developments, as is the mooted summit meeting of homeland leaders, proposed for late in 1973, which could give impetus to moves for a federation of black states in South Africa. (While such a federation would not be able to counter the Republic's economic and military power, it would have considerable bargaining power, particularly with regard to the supply of labour, and it would have influence in the outside world). Arising from the Athlone meeting, mentioned previously, plans are apparently well advanced for another black summit conference, this time to be attended by African, Coloured and Indian leaders.

It is clear that black solidarity has begun to move beyond a purely rhetorical stage to an organisational stage, and that the potential political implications of this are tremendous. Black strikers have mobilised and gained some rewards, and have not been punished for breaking the law. Coloured students have seen the authorities capitulate to some of their demands. SASO has remained militant despite the banning of its entire leadership. Black students expelling white pressmen from their congress is, however limited, an expression of power. Both SASO and the newly formed SASM (South African Students Movement, a grouping of black high school students) and other black agencies such as the Black Community Programmes see clearly the need to move beyond rhetoric and nostalgia to a creative involvement with the black community as a whole, building organisational bases from which that community can move forward to a position of power. Workers, students, political leaders and others have begun to have a taste of that power.

Two recent events have reinforced some of the conclusions in the preceding analysis. First, there was the dramatically successful Ovambo boycott of their 'homeland' elections, followed by a mass SWAPO meeting in open defiance of the law. The second was the renewed unrest at Fort Hare, followed by a total boycott by the student body.

The crisis must increase as the issues become clarified and as the white power structure refuses to bargain on issues like land, freedom of movement, and trade union rights. A neat example of this — and of the way in which the whole white political system is solidifying — was provided by Mr D. Watterson, a United Party leader in Natal. Criticising the central government's proposals for the consolidation of KwaZulu, which will involve the uprooting and resettlement of enormous numbers of people, Mr Watterson is quoted as saying: 'If it was a question of moving hundreds of thousands of whites instead of blacks around, the whites in Natal could be far more energetic in their opposition than they can afford to be now because of the delicacy of black-white relationships today' *(58)*. Stripped of its rationalisation, this means, yet again, do not rock the white boat, since it's the blacks who are going to suffer anyway.

The white political system, embracing all the official parties, is increasingly performing a conserving and restrictive, rather than an innovative, function. Initiatives for change are coming increasingly from extra-parliamentary forces such as the trade union movement and business. Essentially, however, such initiatives are not aimed at fundamental and structural change. It would be absurd to expect *Verligte Aksie* to become a major political force in the whole society, particularly while it is still unable to decide who its constituency should be, what its aims should be (other than vague platitudes), what its strategy should be, and how it should relate to blacks. It may however be able, once it clarifies these matters, to play a useful role by exercising pressure on the entire white political system. Amongst 'liberal' whites re-thinking and re-grouping is also taking place. The insights gained previously by bodies like the University Christian Movement (which played a facilitating role in the emergence of SASO) and NUSAS (which had to respond to the challenges of Black Consciousness sooner than most other whites) are being increasingly expressed in what is called 'a new radicalism' *(59)* or 'post-liberalism' *(60)*, of which some commentators see Spro-cas 2 as the main exponent. If a significant white grouping can emerge based on this 'radicalism', with clear strategies, it could play a valuable role in a future crisis situation. And it could be in a useful bargaining position in a future racial confrontation, with certain insights, skills and resources to contribute.

Among the white Afrikaner ruling group at least two major responses are discernible, with the government shifting rather uneasily to try to accommodate both. On the one hand is the isolationism expressed, for example, by the Afrikaanse-Studentebond, SABRA, the SABC, and some sectors of the Afrikaans Church, who do not wish to be contaminated by exposure to the thinking of others. The trouble with isolationism, a lonely clinging to power, is that, like masturbation, you do not meet interesting people that way. So, for example, a recent survey of the attitudes of young Afrikaners carried out by *The Star (61)* revealed the same tired old stereotypes of their English counterparts ('permissive', 'atheist', 'anti-authority') and of themselves ('Christian', 'conservative in the face of the permissive onslaught' etc). The Afrikaner nationalist press often assists in this isolationism by shielding its readers from the reality of a changing South Africa. The homeland leaders, for example, are presented as puppets manipulated by unnamed 'leftists', there is a diabolical 'liberal conspiracy' (as if liberalism were a potent political force), the rulers of Botswana and other black states are making a hopeless mess, South Africa's blacks are basically contented etc *(62)*.

At the same time, some Afrikaner academics, businessmen and church people are becoming restive. In one issue of *Die Vaderland*, Prof Hennie Coetzee complains about the refusal of a visa to Prof Berkhof, the Dutch theologian, and a columnist complains about the banning of *Cry Rage (63)*.

THE CHURCH

The patterns of inequality and discrimination in the apartheid society are, of course, not maintained solely by the government, and are not embodied only in the great social institutions of education, the economy, the law and the political system. They run deep into the very fabric of the society, in family life and personal relationships, in the workplace, and in the body of the church.

Some of the multi-racial churches 'weight their supreme church courts in disproportionate favour of the whites ... white churchmen have maintained power by packing important committees and commissions of their churches with, and by keeping the highest posts in the hierarchy for, members of their own race ... discrimination between the stipends paid to black and to white ministers in some mixed churches makes these churches sound very hypocritical when they criticise injustice in the civil sphere ... Some of the most scandalous acts of discrimination have been the refusals of white church schools to accept pupils from other races ... The building programmes of white congregations are ordinarily far more ambitious and luxurious than those for black' *(64)*.

A survey by Spro-cas 2 during 1972 revealed that white church schools in the Transvaal paid their black domestic staff an average wage of R36 per month, about half of the Poverty Datum Line for the area. The report on the survey ends with the conclusion that, in general, the church schools show 'an uncritical conformity to white South African standards and an implicit acceptance of the fallacy that blacks need less cash income because their standard of living is lower, whereas, in fact, their standard of living is lower precisely because their income is lower' *(65)*. A subsequent survey of other areas of the country confirmed these findings. Almost no attention was paid to the social and personal needs of the workers, and no provision was made for effective communication with them.

While the distressing implications of this picture remain basically valid a year after the survey and the publication of the Church report, it would be un-fair to discount creative stirrings in the Church. The Anglican diocese of Natal, for example, has agreed to introduce parity of stipends in 1974, several churches have appointed blacks to powerful (and not just token) positions, and several valuable programmes of human relationships and social justice have been attempted. The call has increasingly been heard for a Black Mission to Whites, and a greater understanding and appreciation of Black Theology has been evident in some white quarters.

(The role of the Church as an agency for social change will be looked at in Chapter 4).

CONCLUSION

Earlier in this chapter the statement was made that from birth to death we live in a society characterised by patterns of inequality, injustice and dis-crimination. An attempt has been made to justify this statement, by looking briefly at some of the social institutions in the apartheid society.

Perhaps the most striking indicator of basic inequality, however, is to be found in the life expectancy rates of the different race groups, as given by the Minister of Statistics in the House of Assembly *(66)*:

white women	72,3 years
white men	64,5 years
Asian women	63,9 years
Asian men	59,3 years
Coloured women	56,1 years
Coloured men	48,8 years

The figures for Africans, said the Minister, were not available. Who can doubt, in the light of the grotesque racial hierarchy in South Africa, that they are the lowest of all?

No one who is concerned for human decency, no one who professes any of the great religious faiths, no one who claims to be concerned about the future of our country, can be complacent or apathetic in the face of this picture of white power and privilege and black poverty and frustration.

The challenge of change is a great and difficult one, and the different facets — education, economics, politics — are closely interlocked. Inadequate education perpetuates poverty because it deprives a man of the training needed for a well-paid job. Poverty perpetuates malnutrition and other social ills, which aggravate an inadequate education, and all these things together perpetuate black economic powerlessness.

And all these things help to perpetuate black political powerlessness. And since the distribution of the country's resources — for example, the amounts of money to be spent on the education of the different race groups, or the number of school buildings to be erected — and since the educational policies — for example, the decision that African children should learn three languages in their first year at school, and that the African universities should be sited in remote rural areas — since these things are decided politically, the patterns of discrimination and inequality in our education are politically perpetuated, reinforcing in their turn the other patterns in the broader society.

What more striking example of the importance of political power can there be than the fact that the government plans to spend R470 million for the defence of a social order that breeds resentment and frustration among the bulk of the people? This means that the white parliament has in fact decided — a political decision — to give a higher priority to guns than to schools. This means less of the national wealth is made available to educate those whose education is already unequal and inadequate and who have no participation in the political decision-making process.

FOOTNOTES

1. *Power, Privilege and Poverty*, report of the Spro-cas Economics Commission, p. 13.
2. For example, the Pretoria Medical Officer of Health in his annual report for 1968 reported that the infant death rate for whites was 19,55 per thousand and for Africans it was 107,43 (quoted by H.L. Watts: 'Poverty' in *Some Implications of Inequality*, Spro-cas Occasional Publication 4, 1971).
3. P.M. Leary and J.E.S. Lewis: 'Some Observations on the state of nutrition of infants and toddlers in Sekhukuniland', *South African Medical Journal 39*, 1156, 1956 (quoted by J.V.O. Reid: 'Malnutrition' in ibid.).
4. *Education beyond Apartheid*, report of the Spro-cas Education Commission, 1971, para. 5. 17, p. 24. The data in the rest of this paragraph is drawn from the same report.
5. Ibid., para. 5. 33, p. 29. A Coloured lecturer's salary scale is R2880 - R4080, against his white counterpart's R4200 - R5400 (*Rapport*, 17 June 1973).
6. The Spro-cas Education Report is now out of print, six thousand copies having been distributed. It may possibly be revised and a second edition issued in 1974.
7. Report in *The Star*, 12 July 1973.
8. F.E. Auerbach: *The Spro-cas Education Report - One Year Later* (Spro-cas Background Paper 4, 1972).

9.   Ibid., p. 2.
10. Spro-cas Background Paper 2: *Student Protest - The Conflicting Polarities, 1972.*
11. Ibid., p. 4.
12. Recent events surrounding SASO are detailed in *Black Review* (ed. B.A. Khoapa), published by the Black Community Programmes, 1972, Chapters 12 and 13.
13. F.E. Auerbach, op. cit., p. 4.
14. *Towards Social Change*, report of the Spro-cas Social Commission, p. 15.
15. *Power, Privilege and Poverty*, report of the Spro-cas Economics Commission, p. 20.
16. *The Star*, 5 July 1973.
17. *Financial Mail*, 16 March 1973, p. 944, from which the data in this paragraph is taken.
18. Ibid. p. 947.
19. *Power, Privilege and Poverty*, op. cit., p. 35.
20. Ibid., Appendix D.
21. Ibid., p. 38ff., where this conclusion is substantiated.
22. Ibid., pp. 26-27, from which the data in this paragraph is taken.
23. Ibid., p. 93.
24. Francis Wilson: *Migrant Labour in South Africa*, Spro-cas/SACC 1972, p. ii.
25. John Kane-Berman: *Migratory Labour - the Canker in South African Society*, Spro-cas Background Paper No 3, 1972, p. 2.
26. Jean Le May: 'Down in Phuthadidithjaba', *The Star*, 16 July 1973.
27. It seems that some white farmers actually pay no cash wages at all to their black workers. See report in *Sunday Tribune*, 15 July 1973.
28. *Optima*, July 1973, reported in *Rand Daily Mail*, 18 July 1973, p. 5.
29. *Financial Mail*, 30 March 1973, p. 1159.
30. Ibid.
31. *Optima*, op. cit.
32. *Financial Mail*, op. cit.
33. Ibid., 6 July 1973, p. 46.
34. Ibid.
35. *Power, Privilege and Poverty*, op. cit., p. 60.
36. *Race Relations News*, June 1973, p. 6.
37. Ibid.
38. *The Star*, 13 July 1973, p. 1.
39. *Rand Daily Mail*, 9 July 1973.
40. See *Law, Justice and Society*, report of the Spro-cas Legal Commission, p. 14.
41. S.A. Strauss: Paper on 'Some Basic Values of Our System of Criminal Procedure', Conference on Legal Aid, University of Natal, July 1973, quoted in *The Star*, 5 July 1973.
42. *South Africa's Political Alternatives*, report of the Spro-cas Political Commission, p. 26-27.
43. *Law, Justice and Society*, op. cit., p. 23, p. 72.
44. cf. The Natives (Abolition of Passes and Co-ordination of Documents) Act of 1952: see *Law, Justice and Society*, op. cit., p. 14.
45. By June 1971, about 8 000 whites and approximately 672 000 Coloured, Indian and Chinese people had been forced to move in terms of Group Areas Proclamations, while 200 000 Africans were forced out of 'black spots' and another 175 000 Africans had been removed from white rural areas - study by the S.A. Institute of Race Relations, reported in *Rand Daily Mail*, 9 July 1973, p.
46. Nimrod Mkele: 'Domesticating the African', unpublished paper 1959.
47. *Law, Justice and Society*, op. cit., p. 75.
48. *South Africa's Political Alternatives*, op. cit., p. 21-23.
49. Ibid., p. 22.
50. Ibid.
51. *Die Transvaler*, 18 July 1973.
52. Howard Lawrence: 'Varsity Row a Catalyst for Blacks', *Sunday Times*, 15 July 1973, p. 19.
53. *The Star*, 13 July 1973.
54. *Financial Mail*, 13 July 1973, p. 133.
55. *Rand Daily Mail*, 17 July 1973. It is significant that Chief Mangope is also quoted as endorsing the right of people to support SASO, since it 'is involved in the liberation of the black man'.
56. *The Star*, 16 July 1973

57. *The Star*, 13 July 1973.
58. *The Star*, 11 July 1973.
59. Denis Worrall: *New Nation*, June 1973.
60. *To the Point*, 16 June 1973, p. 32.
61. cf *The Star*, 'The Young Afrikaners', 5 July 1973.
62. See, for example, 'Met wie se stem praat Mangope', *Die Vaderland*, 18 July 1973, and 'Beroep-shulp', editorial in *Die Transvaler*, 20 July 1973, and the fatuous reasons given by *Die Transvaler* (editorial, 3 Aug., 1973) for the successful Ovambo boycott of their separate development elections.
63. *Die Vaderland*, 18 July 1973.
64. *Apartheid and the Church*, report of the Spro-cas Church Commission, pp. 38-41.
65. 'Do Church Schools Exploit Black Labour?' - Spro-cas 2, 1972.
66. Report in *The Star*, 14 June 1973.

The white race tries to minimise the conflict within and between its ethnic groups in order to maximise its efforts to dominate; it also tries to maximise the conflict within and between the ethnic groups of the oppressed black race in order to minimise the latter's resistance in the racial conflict.

Njabulo Ndebele: 'Black Development'
in *Black Viewpoint*, Spro-cas
Black Community Programmes, 1972.

Separation is a reality created by whites, for example through racism in the church, in government and also in our liberal institutions. Through this separatism whites have placed the black man in bondage, in a prison of race. Unknown to himself, the white man has also placed himself in a racial jail — his own racial jail *(1)*.

Horst Kleinschmidt in *White Liberation*,
Spro-cas 2, 1972.

Chapter Two

APARTHEID SOCIETY

THE SOCIAL PROCESSES

IN THE PREVIOUS CHAPTER it was suggested that the present South African patterns of segregation, discrimination, inequality and injustice arise from processes that are inherent in the social system that has developed in South Africa. If one is concerned about changing the social order (and one of the assumptions underlying this report is that Christians must inevitably regard themselves as committed to the quest for social justice and hence as 'active collaborators in change' (2)) then one must move beyond mere awareness of the present position to an understanding of those processes. 'Real change can be achieved only if our analysis is based on an understanding of the origins of the situation and only if we appreciate the complexity of the historical process which has given rise to the present inequality, discrimination and maldistribution of wealth and power in South Africa' (3). Only then can we understand the strength of the fear, prejudice and greed which pattern our society, and only if we have some understanding of these inter-acting forces can we hope to effect change.

Historical Processes

It is not possible for me to attempt a systematic account of the historical processes, but I believe that some of the insights of the Spro-cas Commissions regarding the origins of our present society are illuminating and help us to understand it. Thus, for example, the Economics Commission (4):

> The conflicts between Capital and Labour, English and Afrikaner have been contained by the overriding importance of the black/white cleavage. In the early industrial struggles culminating in the 1922 Rand strike there was a potential for a mobilisation of labour against capital but this conflict was translated over time into a limited conflict between white management and white labour within a context of threat to white dominance from black labour. The underlying alliance between white management and white labour, although uneasy at times, forms part of a fundamental solidarity of all white groups. The English/Afrikaner conflict has also become subordinated to the need for white solidarity. Thus although there are areas of conflict between white groups this conflict is

marginal or is rendered marginal with the result that white supremacy in the political sphere, and white prosperity in the economic sphere, have been maintained *(5)*.

In order to contain the conflicts introduced into South African society by the forces of industrialisation the state has become increasingly powerful. In the economic sphere the white electorate granted steadily increasing powers to the state which was entrusted with the task of maintaining white privilege. The extraordinary powers which Ministers have in determining the economic life of the country must be seen in this light *(6)*.

On the basic question of the distribution of land, the Social Commission considered that:

The difference in technological experience between the whites and the indigenous people also made domination by the whites appear to be 'natural', to some extent even in the eyes of the colonised. White settlers of both British and of Dutch, French and German stock obtained from Bantu-speaking tribes the best land, providing themselves with the initial economic advantage. The land was obtained partly by conquest, partly by land treaties (which whites took to imply ownership, whereas the tribal chiefs probably intended only granting usufruct) and partly by the occupation of temporarily unoccupied land. Deprived of land, many tribesmen had no option but to work as serfs on white-owned land or as labourers in white-owned industry. The need to work for whites was given impetus by the requirement of having to pay poll taxes in cash. Hence ownership of land gained by whites in conquest or by other means must be seen as a very basic factor in the development of the present patterns in South African society *(7)*.

The Church:
The attitudes and motives of Church members in South Africa strongly reflect the situation in the country as a whole, which is characterised by a growing alienation and lack of mutual understanding between black and white people. There are obvious historical reasons for this. Within the Church the evangelisation of black heathen and the pastoral care of white settlers was generally kept separate. The Nationalist government's policy of separate development has furthered and entrenched this separation. Thus while the Church is still one of the few places where black and white can meet in an environment of relative acceptance, for the most part the life of the Church reflects the prevailing social and political attitudes of the country *(8)*.

Migrant Labour:
One hundred years ago, a decade before the birth of the Witwatersrand gold
mining industry, generations before the evolution of the policy of apartheid,
the system whereby men oscillate between their home in some rural area and
their place of work was already firmly established as part of the country's
traditional way of life. During the 1870's, if not before, farmers in the Western
Cape solved the perennial problem of labour shortage — which in previous
centuries had been alleviated through the importation of slaves — by recruiting workers from wherever they could be found. Agents were sent to the
Ciskei, the Transkei, to Mozambique and South West Africa, even as far
afield as Cornwall and Germany, to bring back labourers for the vineyards
and wheatfields of the small colony. In general men were brought to the
farms (and docks) on a contract basis. But many of them, on the expiry of
their contract which varied in length from 2 to 5 years, chose to settle where
they worked and so ceased to oscillate between a distant home and the place
of work. Others, of course, having saved some money and seen the sights
went back from where they had come and did not return ...
... By early 1972, nearly a quarter of a century after the Fagan Report, we find
that instead of the mining and industrial employers having become less
dependent on migrant labour by building family houses for their workers in
town, the manufacturing and services sectors of the economy have become
more dependent upon oscillating migrants who are being housed on a temporary basis in goldmine-type hostels and compounds which are mushrooming
in all the industrial centres of the country *(9)*.

Control of Education:
Until 1954, provincial education departments were responsible for the primary and secondary education of South African children of all ethnic groups.
In the Cape Province, the same inspectors supervised white, Indian and
Coloured schools, and separate inspectors, chosen for their knowledge of the
local African language, supervised African schools. Where there was a common inspectorate there were common syllabuses, common examinations and
examination standards, and persistent endeavours to raise the level of
achievement of the more backward groups to that of the more advanced.
Starting in 1954, in pursuance of the policy of separate development, control
of education for each black race group has gradually been transferred to
separate central government departments, each concerned with only one
group: the Department of Bantu Education, the Department of Indian Affairs
and the Department of Coloured Affairs. There is an emphasis, which is most
apparent in Bantu Education, on separate development and on preparation
for each group's ascribed place in an apartheid system. Centralisation has
been part of the whole machinery of apartheid *(10)*.

Separate Development:
In the 23 years since 1948 it is possible to discern two emphases in the policy
of separate development. On the one hand, decisive moves were taken to
reduce and eliminate such political rights as blacks possessed in relation to
the central parliament, provincial councils and municipalities. The
municipal franchise rights enjoyed by the Coloured people in the Cape for
over a century have finally been extinguished. On the other hand, however,
there have been moves, especially over the past decade, to try and channel
African, Coloured and Indian political aspirations into separate political institutions. In the case of Africans these institutions are territorially-based, in
the sense that they are located in the 'homelands'. Indian and Coloured
people have no such territorial focus and the policy towards them is an
awkward and ambiguous one of 'parallelism' *(11).*

The Law:
The South African legislature, unlike the courts, ignored our liberal tradition
in many important respects well before the advent to power of the National
Party government in 1948. But compared with the inroads which have been
made upon the Rule of Law since 1948 these were trivial. Since 1948 arbitrary
interference with the liberty of the individual has increased alarmingly,
detention without trial has become a permanent feature of our law, and the requirement of equality of treatment for our different racial groups has been
legislated almost out of existence by a host of 'apartheid laws'. Our legislature, particularly in the case of those statutes authorising detention without trials, has built upon a totalitarian foundation which has more in common with the Communist regimes of Eastern Europe or the Fascist system of
Nazi Germany than with our own liberal Roman-Dutch heritage *(12).*

Processes of Control

From these extracts it is apparent that the Spro-cas Commissions generally
agree that one of the basic forces in the present social order is an almost over-
whelming consensus among the ranks of white South Africans, that they
should retain control over the instruments of power and over the major resources of the country, and that the history of apartheid can be interpreted in
the light of this consensus.

Arising from this we get the kind of structural violence inherent in the
social order which was described in the previous chapter. Structural violence
'occurs when resources and power are unevenly distributed, concentrated in
the hands of a few who do not use them to achieve the possible self-realisation
of all members, but for self-satisfaction for the elite or for purposes of dominance, oppression and control ... There are two characteristics of the occur-

rence of structural violence. One, there is not an equal sharing of the fruits of the society, and two, there is not an equal (and equally effective) participation in the making of decisions' *(13)*.

It is possible to regard the high degree of personal and communal violence in the black community as one response to the social hopelessness and the social injustice created by structurally violent conditions and powers, although I accept that the relation between the two is never simple. It is thus possible to regard structural violence as itself functional for the maintenance of the apartheid system with its discrimination and its inequality. A kind of self-perpetuating vicious cycle begins to emerge, if there is any validity in this analysis, along the lines of the perceptive insight by Njabulo Ndebele quoted at the beginning of this chapter. This is not to suggest a conscious design by the white power structure as much as an inevitable outcome of the dynamics at work in the system.

Personal or communal violence 'has its roots in the rage, the fear, the despair, the hate, often self-hate in the hearts of human beings', and these in turn can be reinforced by socially intolerable conditions created by structural violence. Personal or communal violence 'tends to erupt spontaneously in acts which are self-destructive; they may be directed at the wrong targets or perhaps be despairing gestures not linked to any strategy or long-range goal. We see it in the tragedy of physical crime perpetrated by the poor upon the poor. We find it in riots which vent the rage of an oppressed people on any target which is near' *(14)*. South Africa provides much evidence of this kind of self-destructive violence by blacks. Professor van Niekerk believes that the incidence of violence in the black townships or ghettos of South Africa is probably the highest in the world *(15)*.

In Soweto alone there are on average about 80 murders a month, while Baragwanath Hospital treats about 2 000 stabbing cases each month. In one year (1966-67) there were 33 489 cases of theft, 8 075 cases of common assault, 7 747 cases of assault with intent to do grievous bodily harm, 1 156 cases of rape, and 891 cases of murder in the Johannesburg municipal area, the vast majority of these crimes taking place in African townships, especially in Soweto *(16)*. As Professor van Niekerk says, it is difficult to imagine a similar situation being tolerated by the whites in power if the bulk of the victims were white. He also believes that the resulting impression amongst blacks is that the police force serves primarily the interests of the whites in South Africa.

Although apparently rigid, the South African social order is inherently volatile *(17)*. The white oligarchy's determination to maintain its position and the formidably efficient police and military machine are some of the mechanisms that so far have controlled the volatility from erupting into widespread internal insurrection. In looking more closely at the processes of control, the Spro-cas Social Commission has pointed out that the ruling white minority is sufficiently large in relation to the total society to enable all positions of authority in almost every institution to be staffed by whites. This group is also sufficiently large to allow for some competition among whites for positions requiring skill and expertise, and therefore it has been able to maintain adequate standards of efficiency in the administration of the country (although there are recent indications, for example in the postal, transport and health services, of declining efficiency due to a shortage of sufficient skilled whites). The Commission concludes, therefore, that the ruling white oligarchy is in no sense merely a small elitist and unstable ruling clique. White rule is relatively pragmatic and efficient and, in addition, has equipped itself with efficient security services and the most effective modern means of military coercion available, being thereby able to reinforce control by the threat of force and punitive security measures *(18)*.

The positions of authority and control in the state services are generally filled by those deeply committed to the ideology of apartheid. Utterances by military and police leaders reveal this, as do those of people in control of the education of the different race groups. One grievance of the students at the black universities and Colleges of Education is that their Rectors and Registrars are generally nationalist Afrikaners, inevitably committed to implementing the apartheid system.

An illustration is provided by Mr P. W. Prinsloo, appointed by the central government, without consultation with the Indian community, as director of Indian Education. He recently made his views clear: 'Because of basic biological and spiritual differences, racial inter-mixture is extremely risky and dangerous. When two races are mixed, the one is usually dominated by the other and runs the danger of losing its identity completely' *(19)*. Interestingly enough, Mr Prinsloo immediately contradicts himself: 'Apart from scientific (sic) considerations, races as such fortunately also have a sort of self-consciousness and holding back *(weerhouding)* from other races: the negroes of America remain negroes despite the country's enforced integration'. Why then the fear of loss of identity? This sort of specious reasoning is reminiscent of the illogicality of the Tomlinson Commission, which laid down the blue print for separate development in the 1950's. The latter's muddled thinking has been effectively demonstrated by the Spro-cas Political Commission, which concludes by asking: 'Why is it necessary to impose the whole super-structure of apartheid legislation on South African society if it is indeed such a fundamental fact that the white group itself will maintain its 'identity' in the face of all contrary pressures or social change?' *(20)*. Why indeed? Perhaps the reason is that the argument about the preservation of a cultural and/or racial identity is merely a rationalisation for continued dominance and control *(21)*.

After thirteen years of existence, the University of the Western Cape has only 12 black lecturers on its teaching staff of 79. All of the nineteen professors are white (and of these only four have been trained at English-language universities).

The university's supreme governing body, the Council, has only two black members out of a total of 16, while the administration is similarly dominated by whites *(22)*. Essentially the same pattern obtains at the other black universities and colleges *(23)*.

UNIVERSITY OF ZULULAND

Applications are invited from applicants with the appropriate experience for the undermentioned vacancy. The possession of a degree will be a strong recommendation.

REGISTRAR

1. Applications must be accompanied by certified copies of certificates and diplomas and recent testimonials. and must indicate the following:
   1. Degree attained
   2. Experience
   3. Competence in both official languages.

2. **Advantages:**
   1. Housing at nominal rental on the Campus
   2. Group Life Assurance Scheme
   3. Pension Scheme
   4. Medical Aid Scheme
   5. Holiday Savings Bonus
   6. Payment of transport expenses
   7. Generous leave privileges
   8. Territorial allowance.

GENERAL:

1. Full particulars in connection with salary scale and also prescribed application forms are obtainable on request.

2. Completed application forms should be directed to:
   THE REGISTRAR
   UNIVERSITY OF ZULULAND
   PRIVATE BAG
   KWA-DLANGEZWA
   VIA EMPANGENI

Closing date for applications: Friday. 10th August. 1973.

N21   13   SV—578909G

Advertisement in *The Star,* July 13, 1973

This advertisement for the key administrative official of a black university makes it quite clear that only whites need apply (the references to 'territorial allowance' and 'competence in both official languages' — i.e. English and Afrikaans). It is interesting that salary scales are no longer given in advertisements for staff at black state institutions, presumably because of the embarrassment caused by having to reveal discriminatory salaries for white and black. White institutions still indicate their salary scales.

Senior posts in the Coloured Development Corporation, the Bantu Investment Corporation, the Xhosa Development Corporation, Radio Bantu
(which, with its 3 million listeners 'in the Bantu's own language' *(24)*, must
not be under-rated as an instrument of control), the Group Areas Board, the
Decentralisation Board (which functions to re-locate industry in the 'border
areas'), the Bantu Mining Corporation (which deals with the mining industry
in the African homelands) and the regional Bantu Affairs Administration
Boards are all filled by the (white) government from the ranks of white
sympathisers. Since the decisions of these bodies closely affect the lives of
blacks, and since blacks are neither represented on nor consulted by them,
this network of control serves to perpetuate the kind of structural violence described earlier in this chapter.

Advertisement in the *Financial Mail*, July 6, 1973

The Bantu Administration Boards provide a particularly revealing illust-ration of the process. According to the chairman of the West Rand Board, its function is 'to serve the interests of the urban Bantu within the broad frame-work of government policy' *(25)*. (The chairman is, incidentally, the brother of a Cabinet Minister and he is a teacher in a white school). The Minister of Bantu Administration has warned board members that they must follow government policy and not act as mouth-pieces for organisations they repres-ent *(26)*. Presumably he was referring to the United Party members from the Johannesburg City Council on the West Rand Board. This partiuclar board will have control over more than a million Africans in the most densely pop-ulated part of the Republic and its most developed industrial complex. The Cape Midlands Board, under its chairman, Mr 'Boet' Erasmus, embraces 20 local authorities containing 491 000 Africans *(27)*. Despite exhortations by the Minister 'to keep continuous contact with Bantus and Bantu organisations' *(28)* no machinery for this is proposed. Certainly the possibility of 'Bantus' actually being represented on the Boards has been emphatically rejected. Among other matters, these Boards will have power over the movement, employment and housing of Africans under their jurisdiction.

The Boards receive no subsidies from the state, their income being derived from local authorities, 'increased levies from employers and higher rentals in African residential areas' *(29)*. Such income is normally used — for example, the profits received from the sale of 'Bantu beer', which is a monopoly of the local authorities — for services and facilities in the African townships. With the establishment of the Boards an extensive network of extremely well-paid whites comes into operation. The Bantu Administration Board for the High-veld Area has invited applications 'from European persons' *(30)* for sixteen posts, ranging from a Chief Director at R10 200 per annum to a Typist Grade 1 at R2 550 x 150 to R3 000 p.a.

The Bantu Administration Board for the Eastern Transvaal likewise 'in-vites applications from suitably qualified White persons' for six senior posts all of which carry salaries in excess of R10 000 per annum *(31)*. The Central Transvaal Board offers its four senior directors more than R11 000 p.a., with the Chief Director receiving R12 600 p.a. *(32)*. The Northern Transvaal Board makes it clear that 'appointments are subject to the approval by the Minister of Bantu Administration and Development', while offering its chief execut-ives between R9 000 (for an Administrative Control Officer) to R11 200 (for a Chief Director) *(33)*.

The total salary bill for the senior white officials of these four Transvaal boards alone amounts to approximately R285 500 per annum. The pattern is the same in other regions of the country, with local variations (the Drakens-berg Board, for example, throws in a legal adviser at R8 100 *(34)*). By June

BANTU AFFAIRS ADMINISTRATION BOARD
Area: Central Transvaal
PERSONNEL VACANCIES

Applications are invited from eligible persons for appointment to the following vacant positions:—

1. CHIEF DIRECTOR
SALARY PER ANNUM: R12 600 (fixed)

2. DIRECTOR OF LABOUR & COMMUNITY AFFAIRS
SALARY PER ANNUM: R11 400 (fixed)

3. DIRECTOR OF ADMINISTRATION
SALARY PER ANNUM: R11 400 (fixed)

4. DIRECTOR OF FINANCES
SALARY PER ANNUM: R11 400 (fixed).

APPOINTMENT QUALIFICATIONS:
Posts 1, 2 and 3: Appropriate degree and/or experience.
Post 4: Associate Membership of the Institute of Municipal Treasurers and Accountants or an equivalent qualification.

GENERAL:

Five-day week.
Leave bonus.
Compulsory Group Insurance.
Housing allowance.
Medical Fund.

Pension Fund.
Conditions of service

Locomotion allowance as determined by the Board.

Applications must be done in writing with reference to qualifications, experience, age, marital status and telephone number

CLOSING DATE FOR APPLICATIONS: Wednesday, 18th July, 1973, at 12 noon.

Personal canvassing for appointment will disqualify a candidate for appointment. Selection and appointment of candidates is entirely in the gift of the Board.

DR. P. F. S. J. VAN RENSBURG,
Chairman.

Bantu Affairs Administration Board for Central Transvaal, P.O. Box 384, Pretoria.
IvR/MCT.
26th June, 1973.

3   6 SV—378360 (G)

Advertisement in *The Star,* July 11, 1973

1973, twenty-two of these boards had been established, which means that somewhere in the region of R1 400 000 was envisaged as going into the pockets of white officials out of money intended for African administration and development. About thirty fully equipped African primary schools, or 750 classrooms, or school accommodation for approximately 30 000 African school children, could be provided with this money.

That the final salary bill for white officials serving the Boards will be truly astronomical is clear from a recent advertisement placed by the East Rand Bantu Affairs Administration Board *(The Star,* 10/8/73). The Board invites applications from candidates (with standard 10 English and Afrikaans) to fill 18 posts in its Finance Department, ranging from an Assistant Director (R10 800 p.a.) and Chief Accountants (R10 200 p.a.) through computer officers (R8 100 p.a.) and programmers (R6 300 p.a.) to clerks (R4 200 p.a.). The total salary bill for this one department alone excluding the Director, is in excess of R130 000. Since there are generally at least four departments in each board, more than R500 000 must be considered a conservative estimate of the amount involved. And this is only one board, out of a total envisaged of twenty-nine.

The financial inducements for white applicants for such posts are very considerable (particularly since pension benefits, housing and locomotion allowances and leave bonuses are also usually included) and so able people are likely to be attracted who will inevitably feel a loyalty to the government and its policy. The demarcation of the tasks (under each Chief Director there are generally Directors of Labour, Administration and Finances) reveals an extremely effective system of control.

It was perhaps inevitable that one of the first major discussions in the West Rand Bantu Administration Board revolved around the question of a car for the chairman, Mr 'Manie' Mulder. The executive proposed that an 'extravagantly splendid car' costing R12 000 should be purchased for its chairman and the Board decided to debate this in camera (showing some degree of sensitivity to the implications of such a purchase). An editorial in the Johannesburg *Star* commented that 'what makes it worse is that this car is presumably to be paid for out of money intended for African services and amenities — that is the only source of revenue the Act ascribes to the Board. It is bad enough that this money should have to pay the remunerations and allowances of the seventeen or so members of the Board. But their cars too?' *(35).* To his credit Deputy Minister of Bantu Aministration Janson vetoed the purchase of such an expensive car. The next creative move by the West Rand Board — which clearly is destined for great things — was to move its account from Barclays Bank to *Volkskas,* thereby making about R50 million available for Afrikaner enterprises. The same procedure is now being followed steadily by the other boards.

Thousands of whites are living parasitically off the whole complex system of 'Bantu Administration', from inspectors who go about checking that the 'passes' of domestic workers are in order to the handsomely paid directors of the regional boards and their superiors in the Department of Bantu Administration itself. A vast, poorly paid black proletariat is enmeshed in a huge and bewildering bureaucratic machine that determines where they may live, for whom they may work, and indeed, whether they may even live together as man and wife.

TOWN COUNCIL OF BOKSBURG

STAFF VACANCIES

Applications on the Council's prescribed application form, obtainable from the Administrative Assistant, P.O. Box 215, Boksburg (Telephone 52-2571), are invited from bilingual persons for appointment to the following vacancies in the Council's service:—

BANTU ADMINISTRATION DEPARTMENT:

INSPECTOR OF BANTU: (3 Posts)

Salary Scale:
R3 240 x 120—R3 600 per annum plus a 10% salary increase which is in operation as from 1st April, 1973, with a view to a regrading later during this year.

Qualifications:
Std. 8 with 3 years' appropriate experience.

CLOSING DATE:
12 NOON ON WEDNESDAY, 27th JUNE, 1973.

OTHER BENEFITS:
(a) Leave bonus, presently 7½% of annual salary with a maximum of R400.
(b) Housing subsidy scheme, subject to certain conditions, with a maximum of R60,00 per month.
(c) Group Insurance Scheme.

LEON FERREIRA,
Town Clerk.

No. 89/73
Town Hall,
Boksburg.
12th June, 1973.

3   1R SV—576091 (G)

Advertisement in *The Star,* June 18, 1973

This advertisement indicates one aspect of the network of control exercised over the lives of urban Africans. Only whites need apply for such positions. Note the low academic qualification required (Std 8). One task of an 'Inspector of Bantu' will be to apply the pass laws.

The all-pervading patterns of inequality and discrimination in South Africa are supported by the myriad laws and regulations churned out by the bureaucratic machine. Since 1909 some 200 laws have been passed which seek to regulate relations between the races or which are applicable to specific (usually black) racial groups and the number of these laws has progressively multiplied over the years (between 1961 and 1971 no less than 98 laws) *(36)*. It is against this background that the conclusion of the Spro-cas Social Commission should be seen: 'Hence we see that laws in South Africa, in making existing social norms and practices more rigid and authoritative, have made discrimination, inequality, status distinctions and distinctions in privilege so utterly pervasive that these characteristics have penetrated deep into the consciousness of both blacks and whites. If any one factor is to be singled out as accounting for the surface calm and lack of open conflict in South Africa, it is the rigidity and pervasiveness of inequality in the society. In a macabre sense, therefore, the authorities in South Africa are right when they maintain that the myriad laws and regulations are there to preserve 'harmonious' and 'peaceful' relations between the groups in the country' *(37)*. Or, as the authorities are also fond of saying, the laws and regulations are necessary 'to preserve the South African way of life', for that way of life *is* discrimination, inequality and authoritarian control. Or, as they also say, 'to preserve white culture and Western civilisation'. As Professor van Zyl Slabbert points out, if these terms imply 'that the majority of white families should be able to employ poorly paid black domestic servants to do the household chores and help to socialise the children; that white children should go to better schools and universities than black children; that the white entrepreneur should have exclusive rights to obtain property and invest capital in the most profitable industrial sites and have a sufficient supply of unskilled or semi-skilled black labour that cannot effectively organise itself; that only whites should have freedom of access to the best facilities and institutions for their pleasure, education and careers — then the whole argument of 'cultural survival' becomes a tautology. Because then separation is not a pre-condition for the survival of 'white culture', but lies at the very heart of the culture itself' *(38)*.

The Spro-cas Political Commission dealt with the matter from a different angle: 'Apartheid is justified as necessary to reduce racial friction. Good fences, it is said, make good neighbours. There is a plausibility about this argument which renders it attractive. In the South African context, however, it is vitiated because the neighbour with the biggest property decided where the fence should be, how much it should cost, who should pay for it, and who should erect it. Apartheid is not the product of a negotiated agreement between the affected parties — it has been the unilateral decision of the most powerful group in the society, acting with its own interest uppermost in mind' *(39)*.

AFRICAN NOTICES

Situations Vacant (African)

AFRICAN lady badge maker and embroiderer required by Benoni factory (Applicants must reside in that area). To start as soon as possible. Contact Michael at 54-1434 to arrange an interview.

AFRICAN salesman required for a field organisation. Top wages paid to the right men. Apply 38 Fraser-st, Jhbg.

AFRICAN polisher repairer required. Must have spray painting experience. Apply Wolfsons, 38 Fraser-st, Jhbg.

AMBITIOUS YOUNG MEN AND WOMEN

Needed by large American company, to be trained in sales promotion. Please call for interview at World Centre, Shop 14, 48 Railway-st, Germiston, between 9.30 am and 10.30 am.

ANIMAL ANTI-CRUELTY LEAGUE requires a non-European truck driver with a heavy duty licence, able to drive a 10-ton truck. Must be bilingual. Salary negotiable. Tel 26-3966 or 66 Marjorie-st, Regents Park.

COOK/housemaid to live in. Morningside Must have Sandton pass and recent references. Tel 53-8632 after 5.30 pm.

COOK required for aged home. Tel 678-5111 Matron. Accommodation available.

COOK/HOUSEMAID

Very experienced, pleasant person required. Tel 636-7763.

COOK/housekeeper with good references and Sandton pass for Kelvin home of business couple with children at boarding school. Brand-new room with own bathroom. Tel 728-5721, or call at office on top floor Grove Centre, 288 Louis Botha-ave, Orange Grove.

DRIVER

REQUIRED for town and country. Apply with references and licence, 1st Floor, 31 Sherwell-st, Doornfontein.

EXPERIENCED INDIAN AFRICAN OR COLOURED PUNCHCARD OPERATOR WANTED to start immediately. For appointment. Tel 24-3942.

EXPERIENCED driver for private car, required immediately. Jhbg pass and good references necessary. Apply 728-1225.

EXPERIENCED cook/housemaid to start immediately. Sleep in, must have Jhbg pass and refs. Highest wages paid. Apply The Looking Glass, cor Louis Botha-ave, Bramley. Tel 40-3666.

EXPERIENCED nanny/housemaid required. Must have Jhbg pass and recent references. Tel 47-1653.

EXPERIENCED cook/housemaid general. Must have Jhbg pass and recent references. Apply 616-4391. 26 Roll-rd, Cyrildene.

EXPERIENCED driver required immediately. Jhbg pass and good references. Apply 41-4286.

EXPERIENCED driver required with a thorough knowledge of Jhbg and the Reef. Must have clean licence. We offer a 5-day week, good salary. Please call Boutique Fashions, 1st Floor, No 3. Manners Mansions, cor Jeppe and Joubert-sts. City.

EXPERIENCED driver, for commercial traveller in town and Reef. Able to handle sample ranges. High wages paid. Apply in person to 1st floor, Canada House, 90 President-st, Jhbg.

EXPERIENCED, hardworking house/garden boy plus pool for home in St Andrew's. Must have Jhbg pass. Good wages offered. Tel 23-8755 day and 53-2783 evenings, Mrs Ellis.

EXPERIENCED cookgirl, Jewish cooking a recommendation. Must have references. 21a Pretoria-st, Oaklands, 728-2270.

FEMALE DRIVER/COOK

EXPERIENCED woman with Jhbg pass required by elderly lady. Tel 728-4150.

GARDEN/Housemale, experienced with good refs for Rosebank. Good wages, apply to 2 Baker-st, opposite President Place early morning.

GARDENER/House help required. Must have Sandton pass and references. Apply 114 Mattie-ave, Parkmore.

GARDENER required. Middle-aged male required to live in. Please apply in person to 2 Sable-rd, Emmarentia.

HOUSEMAID/cook. Jhbg pass and references. Tel 41-8015 between 9 am and 12 pm.

HOUSE GARDENER

RELIABLE male required for Waverley with pass and reference. Top wages. Apply to Pelemecanique. 61 Booysens-rd, Booysens.

Although this analysis has concentrated on the overt political manifestations of white control (and has not been exhaustive even here — direct
arbitary actions like the refusal of a passport to Mr Hassan Howa, president
of the non-racial South African Cricket Board of Control *(40)*, and the
bannings of SASO, BCP, BPC and NUSAS leaders being another form of control), sight must not be lost of the fact that the economic system is also controlled by the interlocking institutions that make up the white power structure. The great corporations and companies are white-controlled. The
Chambers of Industries and of Commerce, the trade union movement, the personnel and marketing institutes, all these represent other facets of the structural violence which excludes blacks from the major decision-making processes. The communications media fall into the same pattern — not only is
the SABC (and SATV, when it comes) controlled by the state, but, in the final
analysis, the entire Afrikaans press is controlled by the leaders of the
Nationalist Party *(41)*. Of the 24 major newspapers, only three are completely
independent — the *Natal Mercury,* the *Natal Witness* and the *Daily Dispatch.*
The other English papers are owned by two big groups, the Argus Company
and South African Associated Newspapers, whose boards are dominated by
powerful industrialists. These two companies are closely linked, with the
Argus Company owning a third of SAAN. SAAN is now also showing an
interest in acquiring some share of the *Natal Mercury.* As Mr Donald Woods
has pointed out, 'this business of ultimate potential power to control newspapers is obviously an important one, and it is a bigger issue than the
personalities involved ...' *(42)*.

(Despite these cautions, one must express profound admiration for the
majority of the journalists on the English press in South Africa. Without their
constant vigilance and their courage we would be kept in great ignorance of
the true situation. Their constant efforts to expose injustice, racial prejudice
and administrative bunglings are too little appreciated by most South
Africans.).

There is no independent black press in South Africa, and no black-
controlled publishing house. In the USA, blacks soon recognised the importance of controlling some of the media so that they could correct the negative
self-image which blacks had gained from white-controlled media, and it was
inevitable that perceptive blacks in South Africa should now be aiming in the
same direction.

The white-controlled institutional network extends beyond the borders of
the country. Apart from the diplomatic and propaganda machinery created
by the government, there are other agencies busily at work trying to improve
the country's 'image' abroad, while bodies like SAFTO (South African
Foreign Trade Organisation) are seeking to promote the Republic's foreign
trade, and the South African Foundation, for example, has advised British

companies on their evidence before the House of Commons sub-committee into the wages and employment practices of British companies operating in South Africa *(43)*. The Foundation also invites influential people from other countries to visit the Republic, and encourages the formation of sympathetic pro-South African groups abroad.

Control by Insidious Steps

One way in which the South African government seeks to thwart the evolution of a just social order in South Africa has been described in the Spro-cas 2 publication, *Fear or Freedom,* which aimed to alert, in particular, the English-speaking public to what the government is trying to achieve by means of its actions against individuals *(44):*

> In 1959 the Nationalist government attacked and severely injured the English-language universities. In the 1960's it again directly attacked organisations and institutions which enabled people to express opposition to its racial and ideological plans for South Africa. Although these organisations were not illegal, many of them were simply declared so and eliminated. They included all representative black political parties.
>
> The frontal attacks on large organisations aroused widespread public protest within South Africa and attracted unfavourable international publicity for the Nationalist regime. The government has accordingly resorted, since that time, to less direct methods of eliminating legal opposition to its policies. Instead of banning organisations outright, it now bleeds them to death by banning individual members and leaders and thus intimidating others.
>
> This method is slower and less dramatic than the method of direct attack on institutions and organisations. But it is more effective in several ways. Because organisations and institutions are bled to death by many small steps, apparently unconnected, it is much more difficult for the public to become roused against the common political objective which these steps are in fact designed to serve, to see the plan behind them. Because there is no direct attack on institutions themselves, the government can mislead the public by claiming that it is not the institutions it is concerned with, but only certain individuals, who happen incidentally to be associated with those institutions. In this way the Nationalists destroyed the Liberal Party, while proclaiming its right to exist. Similarly, while denying a Church-State confrontation, they continue to weaken and destroy the work of the English-language churches through persecution of many individual churchmen. The same method is now being used against student organisations, university departments, black organisations and trade unions.

The unfortunate people who are selected as victims are isolated from their fellow countrymen by insidious propaganda. There is always talk of 'secret information', which is never produced to the public or the courts. They are stigmatised as 'activists' or 'leftists' and their characters are ruthlessly assassinated by scurrilous innuendoes. They are prevented by banning orders from defending themselves against such smears in any way. Uncertainty, doubt and fear are thus exploited to keep the public divided and to prevent people joining in protest together. And so the process continues, each step only a little worse than the previous ones, but all of them leading ruthlessly in the same direction, the elimination of all organised opposition to apartheid or the National Party.

As Robin Margo has pointed out, the lesson of Nazi Germany is that that one great shocking occasion which will unite everyone in opposition never comes *(45)*, or, as Milton Mayer has said *(46):*

What happened in Germany was the gradual habituation of the people, little by little, to being governed by surprise; to receiving decisions taken in secret; to believing that the situation was so complicated that the government had to act on information that people could not understand, or so dangerous that it could not be revealed for national security reasons. To live in this process did not mean that one noticed it. Each step was so small, so inconsequential, or on occasion so regretted, that unless one were detached from the whole process from the beginning, unless one understood what the whole thing was in principle, what all these 'little measures' that no 'patriotic German' could resist must some day lead to, one could no more see it developing than a farmer sees his corn growing — until one day it is over his head.

Processes of Socialisation

Afrikaner nationalism represents a power group within a power group, and it maintains its position through its control of the political system of the country. Although the 'English' churches are warned to refrain from 'politics' or even the 'social gospel', the Afrikaans churches are willing hand-maids in the service of Afrikaner hegemony. It is not surprising that many political leaders are drawn from these churches, although the admission that politics and religion are inseparable is not usually as frankly expressed as it was recently by Dawie de Villiers M.P., one-time Springbok rugby captain, dominee and academic: 'As a Calvinist I believe that each work must be a calling for one as a Christian' *(47)*. Afrikaner nationalist political supremacy

(basically as a result of the historical accident that Afrikaner whites outnumber the other white groups) is buttressed by a host of political, cultural
and religious bodies all dedicated to this aim. In acquiring political control,
Afrikaner nationalism has also acquired control of the country's education
system, one of the major institutions for the socialisation of the youth of all
races. The way in which this control of the education system has been used to
perpetuate white domination, to ensure the continuation of existing patterns
in the South African population and the retardation of processes of change,
as well as the deliberate use of the system to indoctrinate children with the
belief that apartheid is the only acceptable policy for South Africa, has been
dealt with by the Spro-cas Education Commission *(48)*. In essence, the findings of the Commission suggest that the education system helps to prepare
whites for a dominant role and blacks for a subservient role in the social
order. The finding of the Spro-cas Economics Commission is substantially
the same *(49)*.

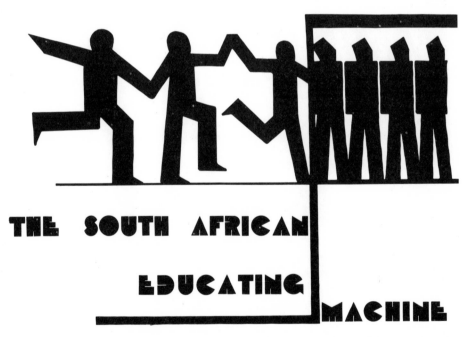

The quest for white conformity, expressed for example through 'Youth Preparedness',
inspired this Spro-cas poster by Rob Collins.

The banning and censoring, with monotonous regularity, of films, books and other material, by the government-appointed Publications Control Board, and the progressive increases in the scope of the Board's operations (for example a Bill which limits appeals to the courts against decisions of the PCB), is a further example of the way in which the state seeks to control the awareness and social consciousness of South Africans, both black and white. (African adults are sometimes not allowed to see films which are passed as suitable for white children).

An illuminating example of the strength of the socialising forces in the apartheid society is provided by a recent study by Professor John Stone of Columbia University of British immigrants to South Africa *(50)*. Professor Stone found that British immigrants drifted rapidly into the structure of South African society and were rapidly acculturated into South Africa's racial norms and dominant values. Only 21 per cent favoured apartheid while still in Britain, but after some time in South Africa the percentage rose to seventy-six. The significant improvement in their standard of living and their economic prospects is clearly one reason for this.

Helping white immigrants to adapt to the system?

The psychological effects of the South African social order on both blacks and whites must be considered. In the first place, 'the various security measures have severely weakened black leadership and for many years a climate of fear has prevailed which has undermined attempts to mobilise under-privileged black peoples' *(51)*.

Some of the findings of the Spro-cas Social Commission are worth quoting in this regard *(52)* (bearing in mind that the Commission's report was written nearly two years ago, before the present development of Black Consciousness, which is aimed at changing the self-image of blacks indicated by this analysis, and which is one of the major potentials for changing the entire social order):

The social divisions between ethnic groups which many of the laws foster also have important effects. It is safe to say that a vast majority of blacks have no contact with whites whatsoever, outside of the formal hierarchical relations in places of employment and in contacts with white police and officials. This tends to create a considerable social 'distance' between whites and blacks. Among many blacks, this seems to have the effect of discouraging comparisons of their own circumstances with those of whites. The whites are remote beings whose position is seen as being 'unassailable'. Among many whites, on the other hand, the rigid social separation creates the impression that blacks live in another society, in another and largely unknown 'world'. As Professor Reid says when writing about poverty and malnutrition among blacks, apartheid creates the impression that blacks live in a world where different standards apply. This cuts the blacks off from a good deal of sympathy from whites who would be very distressed if similar conditions prevailed in their own communities *(53)*. The absence of any cross-cutting social ties between communities keeps whites relatively ignorant of conditions among black communities. Lack of social contact other than master-servant contact and contact in the workplace also perpetuates the 'stigma' of colour in the eyes of most whites. For most whites the notion of any informal contact with blacks, in an atmosphere of equality, is strange and disquieting.

A further feature of South African laws and regulations is that they emphasise racial and tribal divisions among South African blacks in myriad different ways. Job reservation determinations and the facility of asking for more determinations in terms of the Industrial Conciliation Act give Indians and Coloureds a great deal of protection from labour competition from Africans. Hence any sense of a shared position of being discriminated against, of being exploited, is undermined. Furthermore, as in many authoritarian societies, or in societies characterised by vast

social and economic inequality, patterns of interaction are self-rein-
forcing. The wealth, education and confidence of the average white tend
to give him an advantage in any interaction with blacks, which in turn
makes the blacks feel inferior, producing among the latter, low morale, a
lack of self-confidence, dispiritedness and apathy. Thus the psychology
of an oppressed group is functional for the maintenance of the system.

Professor Schlemmer says in the same report *(54)*: 'South Africa's tragedy
is that it suffers from all the ingredients of the social ills of the world combined — distinctions in class, colour, status, language, religion, culture, as
well as having the unfortunate legacy of a relatively recent history of colonial
conquest and wars over territory. In South Africa, these problems are writ
large but they are not qualitatively different from the problems of plural
societies the world over. White South Africans, as an aggregate of
individuals, are no more blameworthy than anyone else. If blame is to be
apportioned, the culprit is 'human nature', or, more precisely, the way in
which human beings tend to be socialised in most cultures'.
   The element of white fear is analysed by the Social Commission in these
terms *(55)*:

Some element of anxiety is probably always present among members of
privileged groups in class societies. Status anxieties and a sense of threat
from lower status groups are fairly typical. In South Africa this type of
fear appears to be accompanied by an even more powerful fear, largely
irrational in nature, arising out of the marked racial differences in the
society. This fear is probably rooted in fairly typical basic anxieties relating to 'identity', and as such is a fairly common human phenomenon.
In many South African whites, however, it seems to assume the form of
an irrational, compelling fear of being 'swamped' — of utter annihilation
— by the black groups which powerfully outnumber whites.
This anxiety is allayed to some extent by compulsive domination. Many
whites feel 'safe' only when they are clearly on top — masters in complete
control of black servant classes. Obviously, this behaviour, which
accords with the social and economic patterns in our society, creates conditions of hostility and resentment among the objects of the domination.
In this sense the irrational identity-fear creates a situation where there
are rational grounds for fear. This reinforces the initial fear and a vicious
cycle results. In addition, the complete domination over blacks must
cause a sense of guilt among many whites. It is not unlikely that this
guilt results in these whites automatically assuming that the blacks they
dominate are hostile and antagonistic.

The Political Commission dealt with the effects of domination upon those who enforce it: 'White South Africans enjoy one of the highest standards of living in the world ... Their privileges and their lack of genuine contact mute their feelings of common humanity and desensitise them to the needs and wishes of those of a different colour ... The rhetoric and the actions aimed at the goal of self-preservation ... create the laager mentality which breeds values that are the antithesis of love, compassion and humanity. Toughness, discipline, obedience and conformity instead become the esteemed virtues when a collective paranoia grips society; and qualities such as individuality, creativity and spontaneity suffer in turn' *(56)*.

This is the racial jail in which the white man has placed himself and in which he is spiritually and psychologically less free than those whom he seeks to dominate.

FOOTNOTES

1. Compare the Spro-cas logo (the crouching naked white man in his box. Ironically enough, the box is open).
2. See *Spro-cas: Five Biblical Principles* (Danie van Zyl, 1972).
3. *Power, Privilege and Poverty*, report of the Spro-cas Economics Commission, p. 46.
4. Ibid., p. 47.
5. It will be noted that this is substantially the same view as held by Ndebele, in the quotation at the beginning of this Chapter.
6. *Power, Privilege and Poverty*, op. cit., p. 55.
7. *Towards Social Change*, report of the Spro-cas Social Commission, pp 22-23.
8. *Apartheid and the Church*, report of the Spro-cas Church Commission, p. 18.
9. Francis Wilson: *Migrant Labour in South Africa*, Spro-cas/SACC, 1972, Chapter One.
10. *Education beyond Apartheid*, report of the Spro-cas Education Commission, p. 37.
11. *South Africa's Political Alternatives*, report of the Spro-cas Political Commission, p. 31.
12. C.J.R. Dugard: 'The Liberal Heritage of the Law', in *Law, Justice and Society*, report of the Spro-cas Legal Commission, p. 24.
13. World Council of Churches: 'Report of the Consultation on Violence, Non-Violence and the Struggle for Social Justice', 20 Nov. 1972, p.6.
14. Ibid., p. 8.
15. B. van Niekerk: 'The Police in the Apartheid Society' in *Law, Justice and Society*, report of the Spro-cas Legal Commission, p. 60.
16. Ibid.
17 See Peter Randall: 'The Present Political Position' in *Anatomy of Apartheid*, Spro-cas Occasional Publication No. 1., 1970, p. 10.
18. *Towards Social Change*, op. cit., p. 7.
19. Address to the Youth Congress of SABRA (the pro-apartheid, all-white South African Bureau of Racial Affairs), reported in *Die Transvaler*, 11 July 1973.
20. *South Africa's Political Alternatives*, op. cit., p. 87.
21. cf. H. Lever: 'Apartheid as Rationalisation', appendix to *Towards Social Change*, op. cit.
22. *Rand Daily Mail*, 23 July 1973.
23. See, for example, *Survey of Race Relations 1970*, S.A. Institute of Race Relations, p. 244.
24. Advertisement in *Financial Mail*, 16 March 1973.
25. *Rand Daily Mail*, 20 July 1973.
26. *Star*, 20 July 1973.

27. *Financial Mail*, 6 July 1973, p. 39.
28. *Rand Daily Mail*, op. cit.
29. *Financial Mail*, op. cit.
30. Advertisement in *The Star*, 18 June 1973.
31. Advertisement in *Sunday Times*, 15 July 1973.
32. Advertisement in *The Star*, 11 July 1973.
33. Advertisement in *Sunday Times*, 8 July 1973.
34. Advertisement in *Die Transvaler*, 12 July 1973.
35. Editorial, *The Star*, 21 July 1973.
36. *Towards Social Change*, op. cit., p. 29.
37. Ibid., pp. 30-31.
38. F. van Zyl Slabbert: 'Cultural and Ethnic Politics' in *Towards Social Change*, op. cit., p. 65.
39. *South Africa's Political Alternatives*, op. cit., p. 30.
40. *Rand Daily Mail*, 14 July 1973.
41. *Cape Times*, 2 Feb., 1973 (report of a speech by Donald Woods at the University of Cape Town Summer School).
42. Ibid.
43. *Rand Daily Mail*, 18 July 1973.
44. Editorial, *Fear or Freedom*, Spro-cas 2, 1973.
45. Robin Margo: 'Loyal Resistance', in *Fear or Freedom*, op. cit., p. 21.
46. Milton Mayer: *They Thought They Were Free*, 1966, quoted by John Kane-Berman in Spro-cas Background Paper 5, 1973.
47. *Die Transvaler*, 11 July 1973.
48. *Education beyond Apartheid*, report of the Spro-cas Education Commission, p. 15. See also the appendix on Christian National Education.
49. *Power, Privilege and Poverty*, op. cit., pp. 41-42.
50. John Stone: *Colonist or Uitlander*, OUP, 1973, reviewed in *The Star*, 12 July, 1973.
51. *Towards Social Change*, op. cit., p. 29.
52. *Ibid.*, p. 30.
53. J.V.O. Reid: 'Malnutrition' in *Some Implications of Inequality*, Spro-cas Occasional Publication 4, 1971.
54. L. Schlemmer: 'Strategies for Change', in *Towards Social Change*, op. cit. pp. 164-165.
55. *Towards Social Change*, op. cit., p. 21.
56. *South Africa's Political Alternatives*, op. cit., p. 29.

The African submits to the white man's demands for deference. He becomes humble in the presence of the white man, takes off his hat when talking to one, gives way in the street to white bullies and never forgets to say *Baas* or *Missus* — and always grins ... How many people have not seen the nauseating spectacle of educated black men sidling up to and trying to ingratiate themselves with white men ... grinning themselves into the white man's favours.

Nimrod Mkele: 'Domesticating the
African', unpublished paper, 1959.

... the Black man must reject all value systems that seek to make him a foreigner in the country of his birth and reduce his basic human dignity. The Black man must build his own value systems, and see himself as self-defined and not defined by others ... before the Black people should join the open society, they should first close their ranks, to form themselves into a solid group to oppose the definite racism that is meted out by white society, to work out their direction clearly and bargain from a position of strength ... a truly open society can only be achieved by Blacks.

SASO Policy Manifesto, 1971.

Chapter Four

CHANGE AND TRANSITION

THE PREVIOUS two chapters have attempted to indicate how the patterns of discrimination, inequality and domination in the apartheid society, as expressed through its social structures, are maintained by a variety of social forces and processes. The white-controlled institutional network's monopolisation of the decision-making processes in the society is a form of structural violence, as defined in Chapter 3.

The Black Strategy

For many years (one could take the establishment of the African National Congress in 1912 as a convenient starting point) the aim of black leaders was to win participation in the white-controlled institutional network which determined the social, economic and political ordering of the society: 'historically their thrust was towards attaining recognition for Africans as equal or potentially equal citizens in a common society' (1). The mass political movements which adopted this strategy reached their zenith in the 1950's. The white power structure effectively resisted the intentions of blacks to participate in the institutional network and, instead, succeeded in systematically stripping away the rudimentary political and civil rights which they had previously enjoyed. In the words of the Spro-cas Political Commission, it is not surprising that after 1961 some African political leaders despaired of attaining their ends by peaceful and lawful means and resorted instead to violence, including the use of guerilla tactics.

Although there are still 'moderate' blacks (or 'non-whites', as the exponents of Black Consciousness label them) who wish to pursue the old strategy of finding acceptance in the white-controlled institutions, it is clear that the major thrust has now shifted dramatically into a new strategy. In 1959 Nimrod Mkele was merely expressing popular sentiment when he described those blacks who had any truck with separatist apartheid institutions as 'the beggars-after-favours in the Advisory Boards, the Bootlickers in Bantu School Boards and Bantu Authorities' (2). The new strategy is itself a 'separatist' one, aimed essentially at the creation of a black institutional network as a counter to white domination. The strategy has been expressed by a number of black spokesmen (3). Bennie Khoapa has put the issue very plainly (4):

It is not 'separation' of blacks but the separatism of whites which threatens this country. The decision is in the hands of whites. If they want transformation, let them give up their separate neighbourhoods and institutions and organisations and come out in the open. Until then, blacks must organise and use their group strength to wrest control of every organisation and institution within reach.

Bennie Khoapa clearly does not believe that the whites will voluntarily 'give up their separate neighbourhoods and institutions and organisations' and as a consequence 'the oppressor and the oppressed must clash'. While some may try to avoid the exigencies of the situation 'by preaching universal brotherhood', this is merely 'a mystification in a situation of oppression'. The main concern of black people at the present time, therefore, is not the fictitious choice between 'integration' or 'separation', but the need for liberation. 'What people call separation in the black community is not separation but regroupment. It is not separation for blacks to come together on matters of common policy. It is not separation for blacks to go on Sunday to a church which has never been closed to anyone'. Recognising that a pre-condition of liberation must be unity, and that black unity in turn requires black organisation, one practical implication of the new strategy is that 'we need more, not fewer, black organisations, we need black-oriented or black-based youth camps, centres, colleges, welfare organisations etc' *(5)*.

The development of black organisations over the past five years has indeed been remarkable. The Black Community Programmes have carried out a survey of the organisational network in the black community and have been able to identify more than seventy cultural, educational, political, professional, religious, self-help, student, welfare and youth organisations *(6)*, whose policy-making bodies are black-controlled. Amongst the most significant black organisations to have been established, and to have taken root, over the past few years have been *(7)*:

ASSECA	—	Association for the Educational and Cultural Advancement of African People (founded 1967)
BAS	—	Black Art Studios (1972)
BAWU	—	Black Allied Workers' Union (1972)
BCP	—	Black Community Programmes (1972)
BPC	—	Black Peoples Convention (1971)
BWP	—	Black Workers' Project (1972)
ELEC	—	Edendale Lay Ecumenical Centre
MDALI	—	Music, Drama, Arts and Literature Institute (1972)
NWA	—	Natal Workshop for African Advancement (1972)

SABTU   —   South African Black Theatre Union (1972)
SASO   —   South African Students' Organisation (19(

Common to all of these has been an espousal of the concept and the strategy
of Black Consciousness, 'a three-year old movement which is rap: ᵈly becoming one of the most powerful forces for change in South Africa. The
phenomenon is clearly much more than political; it represents a culture re-
discovering itself and beginning to assert itself. Thus it reaches beyond the
influence of the African political movements of the '50's which the government effectively crushed. It reaches beyond the aims of politically aware and
articulate blacks toward the very heart and dignity of black culture. Its latent
power is tremendous and probably cannot be crushed, although its growth
might be slowed' *(8)*. One strong element in black consciousness is its rejection of many white values and attitudes, such as competitiveness, acquisit-
iveness and materialism, which have led to the moral and physical violence
of South African society. 'Black Consciousness is not an anti-white philosophy. One is forced to emphasise that it is anti-white values' *(9)*. Black Consciousness will, of course, be in a state of tension with the 'embourgeoisment'
of urban black society, which is helped along by the concentration of the
'black' (but white-controlled) press on 'tycoons', 'socialites' and material
success generally. The theorists of Black Consciousness stress values like
communalism, creativity and spontaneity.

One of the components of the drive towards black organisational development has been the 'Buthelezi strategy' of working from within government-
created institutions like the Bantustan governments, with such associated
tactics as the holding of summit meetings between homeland leaders and the
movement towards a federation of black states in Southern Africa to counter
to some extent the power of the white-controlled Republic. Dr Manganyi has
described this as 'a political dialectical feat of immense proportions, given the
fact that the separate development system they operate within aims at ethnic
fragmentation'. At a different level there is the preparedness of some blacks
sympathetic to Black Consciousness to operate within the separate black
educational and other institutions, and within the Urban Bantu Councils
and other rudimentary forms of local management, presumably with the
intention of ultimately wresting control of 'every organisation and
institution within reach'. James Matthews has expressed one reaction to this
hope *(10):*

Dialogue
the bribe offered by the oppressor
glitters like fool's gold
dazzling the eyes of the oppressed
as they sit around the council table
listening to empty discourse promising empty promises
beguiled by meaningless talk
they do not realise ointment-smeared words
will not heal their open wounds
the oppressor sits secured with his spoils
with no desire to share equality
leaving the oppressed seeking warmth
at the cold fire of
Dialogue

The purists within SASO and some other organisations reject this strategy in toto, arguing 'that the architects of the system know it best and hence are always ahead of any black infiltrators in terms of planning' *(11)*. The tensions in this situation can give rise to dynamics of considerable political significance:

> ... as time goes on, the pressures on homeland leadership will increase and so will the associated frustrations and conflicts. Outside the remote possibilities of despair and indifference, the probable general effect will be that of politicising the present and future homeland leadership. Of added significance is the fact that pressures on the leadership will grow in the homelands themselves outside South Africa's urban areas. During the Richard's Bay strikes of 1973, workers demanded a meeting with a representative of the KwaZulu government. There are visible signs that it is now the ordinary worker who says that the homeland leaders must rise to the occasion, which in practice means a confrontation with South African whites *(12)*.

It would be foolish for whites to take too much comfort from the apparent divisions and tensions between the different exponents of black solidarity. We are witnessing an inevitable historical movement whose own internal dynamics, such as the interplay indicated by Dr Manganyi in the extract quoted above, will help to give it vitality and strength. And while the ideological and strategic issues are debated and clarified, a broadly based movement is emerging for black organisational development across the ethnic and tribal divisions which the policy of separate development seeks to perpetuate. The report of the first national congress of the Black People's Convention, held in December 1972, indicates the tangible concerns of such a movement: within the context of 'the total involvement of the Black Community irrespective of tribal or ethnic barriers', the congress concerned itself, among other matters, with the work being done in the establishment of an independent Black National Bank, and of a national Black Workers' Council; it mandated its officials to organise black leadership training courses, to devise youth programmes directed 'at re-orientating their basic values towards Black Consciousness and Black Solidarity', and to investigate the possibility of adult education schemes; and it called for the creation of independent black sporting organisations *(13)*.

As indicated previously in this report Black Consciousness and Black Solidarity are moving rapidly into an organisational phase after the early rhetoric-filled stage, and the future shaping of our society will be influenced greatly by the degree of success which is achieved.

Conflict and Confrontation

Against this background, it is useful to consider some of the major conclusions of the Spro-cas Commissions on the problem of socio-political change in South Africa. In the first place, there is the recognition that conflict and confrontation have now become inevitable in the process of change. The stage has been set 'for a long and no doubt acrimonious process of collective bargaining on the future of South Africa. It seems that the whites have kept race in the centre of South African politics for too long. Now the proponents of apartheid have finally created the settings in which the blacks will respond to the challenge' *(14)*. One of the arenas for this process of collective bargaining will be the very platforms created by those who implement apartheid as an ideology. These platforms will serve to mobilise 'support and loyalties in terms of racial awareness and not primarily ethnic awareness'. One implication of this is that race 'cannot be ignored or wished away in politics or future political developments in South Africa', since structures have been created that will increasingly operate on a racial basis. Another implication is that 'group politics as opposed to individual political participation will increasingly become more significant in South Africa'. (It was a recognition of this implication that caused the Spro-cas Political Commission to devote much of its efforts to a consideration of the position of groups, as opposed to the 'traditional' liberal concern for the individual only). The Social Commission agreed with the views of Prof. van Zyl Slabbert, quoted above: 'It would seem that the quest for equality will be carried out under the banner of race. Although secure predictions cannot be made, it seems not unlikely that the resolution of this conflict will take the form of some type of bargaining or confrontation between institutions representing racial interests' *(15)*.

The potential for major conflict is very great:

What emerges at present, however, is a picture of a society in which divisions in power, bureaucratic authority, occupational status, social status and standard and style of living — all the factors which constitute or relate to class — correspond almost completely with differences in official ethnic-group membership. Fundamentally, South Africa is a society characterised by deep class cleavages and by a potential for bitter class conflict. It needs to be noted, additionally, that the 'classes' in South Africa, by virtue of their ethnic identity and the laws and social norms which make it virtually impossible for members of one ethnic group to become assimilated into another group, have a 'caste-like' character *(16)*.

When the Social Commission issued its report at the end of 1970, it felt that it was impossible, at that stage, 'to say whether the major lines of race-conflict will be drawn between whites and all blacks collectively, or primarily between whites and Africans with other groups in a marginal position. Trends in both directions can be discerned' *(17)*. Since then the picture has clarified considerably, with the Coloured group moving significantly towards identification with the black cause *(18)*. It is significant that the present President of SASO, Mr Henry Isaacs (banned in July 1973), is a student at the (Coloured) University of the Western Cape, and that two of the SASO leaders banned in March 1973 were Indian. Mr Adam Small has warned of the polarisation that is occurring, with Coloured people increasingly regarding themselves as black as they are on 'the side of the oppressed' (he also attacked 'the materialism and spiritual decadence' of the white power structure). In the 'massive racial confrontation' that is fast approaching, he clearly indicated that the Coloured group would align itself with the blacks against 'the oppressive white structure' *(19)*. It is presumably a recognition of this danger facing the whites that has caused Mr Theo Gerdener, a former Nationalist Cabinet Minister, to form a new political party to accommodate whites, Coloureds and Indians to strike 'a power balance which would obviate a clash between whites and (all) blacks' *(20)*. This is probably also one motivation behind the decision of *Verligte Aksie* to open its membership to blacks *(21)*.

The moves towards an over-arching black solidarity must obviously also be seen in relation to potential tensions between African, Coloured and Indian groups, and the frank admission by some Indian and Coloured leaders that the system favours them relative to Africans. Perceptive white politicians can be expected to try to exploit these situations. 'There is always the possibility that in order to maintain itself in power ... the white group will permit or even seek integration with the minority groups, creating a non-black alliance against the Africans' *(22)*. The setting up by the government in 1973 of a Coloured-white commission into the future of the Coloured people may be a pointer in this direction. It remains to be seen whether the 'brown minorities' are indeed to be actively wooed into a common non-black camp, and, if so, whether this would effectively counter the movement towards Black Solidarity. In the meanwhile, 'the institutions both evolved and imposed in the minority groups may well contribute towards change through becoming vehicles for the expression of group feeling, even violent frustration, and by their demonstration effect' *(23)*.

The views of Mrs Fatima Meer in 1970 are interesting as an indication of a general attitude in the Indian community at that time *(24)*: 'The Indian believes his position to be the most precarious of all in South Africa. He has today reached a point where he considers Afrikaner nationalism, which he knows, as preferable to African nationalism, the only apparent alternative, which he does not know, and about which he hears gruesome stories'. In how far this might represent a general view amongst Indians in 1973 cannot be established without research, but clearly a polarisation process is occurring in this community as well, with some desiring co-operation with government (for example, through the South African Indian Council) in order to obtain concessions (like the recently announced improvements in the rights of Indians to move from one province to another), but with others rejecting this approach and aligning themselves with the forces of Black Consciousness and Black Solidarity.

The Extent of Conflict

The preceding analysis has clearly suggested that

> the potential for conflict between the different race groups is very real and threatening. The question is not whether there will be conflict or no conflict, but rather what the intensity of the friction or conflict will be. Is localised structured conflict in limited sectors of our social life not more manageable than, and preferable to, a situation of polarised unstructured large scale conflict? Is the perhaps painful adjustment process in a work situation where attempts are made not to discriminate in terms of salary, authority and facilities (a situation of localised interpersonal conflict) not more controllable and in the long run more educative than one that polarises anatgonisms and reinforces stereotypes throughout society? Can legislative measures not be used as effectively to combat prejudice and ignorance as to promote it?

If the answers to some of these questions are in the affirmative then the ideological justification for apartheid's separation component is not very convincing. By saying this one is in effect asking: what is the real reason for the separation between white and black? What does this separation mean for white and black respectively? What is the price to be paid for the absence of friction promised by separation? Would it not be more realistic and honest to admit that a number of legislative measures have been inherited and created which patently structure privileges to the advantage of the whites, rather than piously to justify them on the grounds that they prevent conflict? In the last analysis it becomes a choice between the type of conflict that will arise when a more equitable sharing of these privileges is brought about, and the type of conflict that could arise when it is attempted to withhold these privileges indefinitely. A more disturbing question is, of course, whether we still have this option *(25)*.

Conflict of some kind, whether it arises from effective pressure backed by serious threats (which may be the position that homeland leaders are edging towards) or of more open confrontation (which seems now to be becoming a widely held expectation in South Africa, with some whites adopting a kind of war psychosis) will probably precede any significant change. The great danger — against which moderates, both black and white, have been warning for a long time, until the urgency of their warnings has become somewhat muted *(26)* — is 'that internal pressure will take the form, ultimately, of open and unregulated conflict' *(27)*. The enormous gap in wages and living standards, which generally coincides with the racial division, coupled with the fact that the absolute gap in incomes has in fact tended to widen rather than narrow over past decades, 'suggests that when conflicts do emerge ... they are likely to be sharper than those which have occurred in countries where rather more of a gradation of material rewards existed *(28)*'.

The conclusions arrived at by Professor L. Schlemmer in the light of this analysis are very important *(29)*:

> In regard to the prospects of ultimate civil disorder, South Africa might be very much involved in a race against time, as it were. If the system can become significantly less rigid before blacks, particularly Africans, develop a political coherence and organisation, the heat of conflict is likely to be reduced. If Africans face the same intransigence as they face today when their political consciousness has developed, the degree of conflict could be considerable. It seems utterly crucial that the aim of

working for conditions which will reduce the heat of inevitable conflict in South Africa be one of the major goals of strategic action for change. One very broad strategy in itself, is communicating to white South Africans the imperative need to avoid greater tragedy later by working for ameliorative conditions now.

The greatest hope for peaceful change in South Africa lies in the possibility of there being opportunities, in the not too distant future, for blacks to exert constructive pressure on whites and within white-controlled institutions. In South Africa the latent potential for ultimate violence can only be dissipated by institutionalised and regulated 'conflict', in the course of which blacks can press for specific rights and improvements in their circumstances. South Africa's future cannot be safeguarded by constant attempts to deny the legitimacy of black grievances, or by using repressive measures to stave off the time when these grievances will be openly expressed. Organised and regulated bargaining between blacks and whites, commencing as soon as possible, will provide the greatest guarantee of reasonable stability for South Africa in the long run.

In the long run, the crucial question must be the extent to which the white power structure is prepared to bargain on basic issues. The Spro-cas Political Commission has discussed the question of bargainable issues, warning that 'the implications for the conflict potential of divided plural states will be obvious: once ethnic and racial differences become salient they readily provide non-bargainable issues par excellence. What is more, they can easily become impacted with the inherently more bargainable economic differences and thus complicate the chances of rational negotiation on these issues as well' *(30)*. A recent warning in the Afrikaans press supports this view: 'There are certain matters which cannot be negotiated — on which no nation (*volk*) and no community can negotiate ... In South Africa this concerns specifically the maintenance of an own identity. This means that any direction or any tendency which can lead to the abdication of own political rights is unacceptable' *(31)*. (For 'own' read 'white'.) This could, for example, be taken to include the entrenchment of the industrial and social colour bar, the question of corporate bargaining rights for blacks (since this might well be seen to threaten white political power), the question of defence forces for the homelands etc. It certainly includes the franchise within a common political system. The greater the determination of the white power structure not to bargain on such issues, the less likelihood there is of relatively peaceful change.

Change Through Economic Growth?

The Spro-cas Social, Economic and Political Commissions are emphatic in rejecting the facile belief that economic growth of itself will bring about major changes in South Africa *(32)*. They point to the fact that despite the tremendous extent of industrialisation and the economic growth that has occurred since World War 2, the basic patterns of poverty and inequality have remained entrenched and the gap in incomes between black and white has in fact widened. It is possible that some sectors of the black community have actually become worse off than they were before the period of rapid industrialisation *(33)*. Even the shortage of skilled white manpower which has resulted in the absorption of blacks into positions formerly occupied solely by whites — with the usual South African stratagems whereby, for example, black shunters on the Railways are called 'train marshallers' and are paid less than their white counterparts *(34)* — has as yet resulted only in marginal change, since 'the white monopolisation of power operates to maintain white privilege while denying a just reward to blacks' *(35)*. Since economic growth in South Africa operates within the constraints of the social and political framework, this effectively curtails the dynamic for change which industrialisation per se can bring about. Even the fact that Africans have moved with increasing rapidity from the labouring categories into semi-skilled and skilled occupations over the past ten years *(36)*, must be seen against recent findings that 38,3 per cent of the five million economically active Africans are still in agricultural work (the percentage of whites has decreased over the past decade from 6,9 to 4,4, Coloured from 7 to 3,3, and Asians from 0,6 to 0,3), while the number of blacks (all groups: African, Coloured and Asian) in administrative and managerial occupations has decreased since 1960. In the same period, the number of whites in these jobs has risen from 57,003 to 69,850 *(37)*.

Despite these cautions, however, it seems clear that economic forces are crucial in any consideration of the possibilities of major change in South Africa. On the one hand there is the possibility that improvements in the status of black workers may result in a 'revolution of rising expectations' *(38)*, which, if continually frustrated by the constraints of the socio-political framework, may find violent expression. The way in which rising costs more than offset wage gains by blacks, and the increasing exploitation of blacks as consumers, could be additional factors in such a process *(39)*.

On the other hand there is the increasing recognition by white business that accommodations to the country's labour structure are required if white prosperity is to be maintained and if a peaceful future is to be ensured. Even the *Afrikaanse Handelsinstituut (40)* recognises that 'we have become more economically integrated', that 'our economy is now largely dependent on the labour of more than five million urban Bantu', that decentralisation to border industries has had negligible effects and that only R24 million has been spent in ten years on African homeland development (against more than R2 000 million on defence in the same period). While the *Handelsinstituut* offers no practical suggestions, other than a call to the National and United Parties to reach consensus on economic and political problems, other employer organisations have actively canvassed such matters as trade union rights for blacks, the rate for the job and the ending of job reservation. While this may be motivated more by self-interest than concern for black workers, and while the efforts of white businessmen are unlikely to bring about a major redistribution of power and wealth, they do add certain dynamics to the sensitive area of black labour which is crucial in terms of change.

The wave of strikes by black workers at the beginning of 1973 undoubtedly stimulated much of the reformist zeal displayed by some white employers. The Spro-cas Political Commission considered the question whether such economic action could have political effect, i.e. 'could the black population, by using its economic bargaining power, exact political concessions?' The Commission pointed out that in the past there have been other occasions when blacks have gone on strike, as for example on the gold mines in 1946, and in 1960 when nearly the entire African labour force in Cape Town struck for nearly two weeks after Sharpeville. In neither case were political advantages gained. While a country-wide general strike would undoubtedly produce significant political results (whether or not the state resorted to massive coercion), the problems of large-scale organisation and the accumulation of substantial strike funds to support strikers and their dependents for at least a month would make such a strike extremely difficult to accomplish *(41)*.

The white power structure is at present sufficiently strong to accommodate the kind of sporadic action by black workers that will probably recur from time to time in the near future, and the state will probably continue to move systematically against potential growth points of black worker power (as it did through the banning of leaders of the Black Allied Workers' Union and the Black Workers' Project in March 1973, and as it did previously through destroying SACTU, the South African Congress of Trade Unions, in the 1960's), and the activities of bodies like the Universities' Wages Commissions will continue to be smeared by government propaganda agencies. The conclusion of the Spro-cas Economics Commission is that the black worker's only hope is to recognise that although he has ro *legal* bargaining power, he has bargaining power, and that the history of trade unionism shows that workers must first demonstrate their inherent bargaining power before it is legally recognised *(42)*. The educative work of various agencies concerned to train black workers in trade unionism and the astonishing degree of successful organisation (given their massive disadvantages) by black workers in the strikes of 1973, indicate that the long and inevitably painful movement to build black worker's bargaining power is under way.

Although economic development may reinforce the existing social order in the short run, 'it also undermines it in the long run' *(43)* since it results in blacks acquiring more and more strategic positions in the economy and it reinforces the inter-dependence of the races. While the movement by blacks into such positions also gives them a greater scarcity value in the eyes of white employers, 'it is only when blacks can put their occupational status to good effect by becoming organised for hard bargaining in the labour (and ultimately political) sphere that the process will be complete' *(44)*.

A strategy for change which utilises these possibilities and which is based on the considerations mentioned earlier is suggested by Professor Schlemmer in the Spro-cas Social Report. It is important to bear in mind the dynamics which exist within a situation where the urban black proletariat is increasingly consumer-oriented, where many whites see the need to create a 'contented black middle class', in the hope that such a class could act as a counter-revolutionary buffer, but where 'there is no inherent conservatism among rising members of a subordinate class; on the contrary it was this group which initiated and led most historical uprisings' *(45)*.

With regard to trade unionism, one crucial question is whether African workers (the only group who cannot form or join legally recognised unions) will opt for an over-arching all-black union (such as envisaged by Kadalie's Industrial and Commercial Workers' Union of the 1920's *(46)* and, more recently, Drake Koka's Black Allied Workers' Union) or whether they will go along with recent moves by white unions affiliated to TUCSA to form black unions (no doubt spurred on by the potential threat to themselves posed by the first alternative). The philosophical basis for an all-black workers movement has been expressed as follows: 'The classical western elements of trade unionism have to be modified to accommodate the fact that black worker interests extend beyond the factory; they extend to the ghetto where black workers stay together in hostels under squalid conditions; to the crowded trains and buses ... to the absence of amenities ... to the stringent, irksome and humiliating application of influx control laws ... to lack of proper channels whereby people could equip themselves with basic skills ... Black workers are beginning to realise how the system rests squarely on their shoulders while giving back just enough to enable them to come to work the following day ...' *(47)*.

The political implications of a general black union are clearly immense. Paradoxically enough, government policy increases the possibilities for black workers to organise, as for example through the operation of the con-tract system (migrant labour) and the housing of men in hostels where com-munication can occur rapidly and privately. Despite its repeated vehement rejection of trade union rights for Africans, the South African government may well come to believe that white supremacy is less likely to be threatened by allowing African workers trade union rights within existing unions, thus fragmenting the labour force, than by the otherwise possibly inevitable growth of a general black union. Either way, significant dynamics for change will be created.

'The Hidden Association'

The main stress in this report so far has fallen on the divisions in the society, on the forces that increase polarisation and potential conflict. This is inevitable in the context of the apartheid society. Despite the emphasis on apartheid, separate development and the growth of white consensus on the one hand and of black solidarity on the other, the crucial element of inter-dependence between the race groups (or the castes, if this is found to be a useful term) must never be lost sight of as one dimension in any analysis of the forces of change. The Spro-cas Political Report has indicated how it is possible to regard South Africa as in fact an integrated society, in which decisions affecting all are taken by one central government but where an attempt is made to resolve internal tensions through the creation of political sub-systems which, however, remain an integral part of the total system, held together by a common economy.

There are clearly integrative forces in the society: for example economic inter-dependence, 'the affiliation of a majority of the total population to common religious denominations, and the growing practice by large numbers of all races of many elements of a common culture' *(48)*. The old liberal belief that this situation, if left to develop 'naturally', would result in a harmonious common society, has been effectively criticised by the Spro-cas Political Commission. There are, however, several factors in terms of change which may be considered: cross-cutting affiliations between individuals from the different groups could play a valuable role in reducing conflict, and meaningful inter-racial contact could reduce hostile stereotypes. The stress must be on 'meaningful', because, as Professor Lever has pointed out *(49)*, inter-racial contact for its own sake can have the effect of reinforcing negative racial attitudes, as can contact that perpetuates the master-servant relationship (this may be one of the problems at the black universities, where many white liberals had hoped that the meeting between black students and a predominantly Afrikaner staff would lead to a softening of racial attitudes on the part of the latter).

When individuals (or groups of individuals) from the different races are able to confront each other as equals, in situations into which inequality is not structured, and where the self-interest of each requires some readiness to bargain and to accommodate, then meaningful inter-action can occur. This is one of the assumptions underlying Black Consciousness, and it needs to be understood more clearly by white liberals, particularly within the Church, who become very confused because they cannot recognise or accept that confrontation may well be necessary before meaningful reconciliation can occur. In the process, whites must lose any pre-conception that reconciliation has to be on their cultural terms, i.e. that blacks automatically desire to be acculturated and assimilated into their particular value system and cultural mores *(50)*.

The previous section has been something of a digression away from a consideration of the implications for change of the inter-dependence of the race groups in South Africa. Mr L. Douwes Dekker has coined the useful phase 'hidden association' in this connection *(51)*. He points out that any industrial society must result in the creation of numerous goods and services — the road system, ESCOM, water supplies, retail associations etc — which are common to and needed by all people in the community. Industrialisation also brings common needs: preventative health measures, control of pollution, consumer protection etc. All this suggests 'a new form of sociability' which, paradoxically, allows the great potential for individualisation in modern society. 'The more that people use individual goods, the more they are dependent on the community service for common goods'. For example, the more individual cars there are, the more essential is an effective road system. The more electrical applicances allow women to express their individuality by liberating them from housework, the greater their dependence on the common electricity service. (It is calculated that black car-owners will outnumber white by 1999, and steps are now being taken to install electric stoves in all Soweto houses, because the pollution caused by the present coal-burning appliances affects white as well as black Johannesburgers).

This social inter-dependence should mean that all people in the community should have a certain awareness of their common interests, but in South Africa this is denied by the emphasis on 'separate development'. For example, separate post office entrances attempt to deny the fact that the postal service is a common good. Where costs make such 'separation' impossible, a common system operates, as with the road system.

But behind the facade of separation 'the hidden association' is a reality, and constantly has to find expression, whether through multi-racial sports meetings, or joint meetings of racially segregated welfare societies. As industrialisation increases so the hidden association will increasingly have to come into the open, and conflict will arise where it is denied expression. Whites need to see this issue clearly and not constantly seek to deny that it exists or to gag it with tortuous rationalisations. As Mr Douwes Dekker says, 'all parties participating in the hidden association must be given a share in the control of the administrative machinery and decision-making function, and hence in organisations responsible for this unseen association'. The implications for the white-controlled institutional network are clear. The crises that some of the organisations have faced or are facing as the hidden association asserts itself — from the Automobile Association to TUCSA — are described by Mr Douwes Dekker in his chapter. The Church itself is increasingly facing crises on the same issues, from the challenges being posed to the white 'mother' church of the DRC by its 'daughter' churches, to the internal problems besetting some of the multi-racial 'challenge groups' in the Anglican Human Relations Programme. Where there is a ready acceptance of the principle of shared participation, the crises usually do not develop to a point of complete breakdown.

If the 'black strategy' for change outlined earlier in this chapter itself seeks to deny the existence of the hidden association in South Africa it will inevitably face a series of crises in the long run. The tension between the hidden association — the common need for goods and services — and the development of black initiative will be one of the major features in the process of social change in South Africa.

Perhaps John Donne said it all in a different way, a long time ago: 'No man is an island, entire of itself: every man is a piece of the continent, a part of the main ...'

White Consciousness

White consciousness is a relatively recent concept in South Africa and has been promoted particularly by the white programmes of Spro-cas 2 *(52)*. It arises in part from the need of whites who desire meaningful social change to find a relevant role. Such whites are aware that the major initiative for and implementation of such change will come from blacks. It is in part a response to the challenge posed by black consciousness and black solidarity.

White consciousness implies a coming to terms with the fact of being white and the inevitably privileged position this gives one in a society structured to maintain white power and privilege. It means overcoming the paralysing feelings of apology and guilt which tend to make white liberals gloomy and ineffectual protagonists of change. It means being radical in the sense of going to the roots of the problem and dealing with the basic issues of power, wealth and land. Spro-cas has attempted to play a role in the practical working out of such an approach, by seeking to prepare whites for meaningful change, by supporting black initiative where possible, and by helping other whites to react creatively to black initiative.

White consciousness means being aware of the injustice and oppression of the present social order, and of the fact that it damages whites as well as blacks, locking them in a prison of racism, authoritarianism, intolerance and fear. It implies a recognition of the need for white liberation as part of the liberation of the whole society. It means working to influence the attitudes of whites in a liberatory direction, and to modify those structures controlled by whites which are amenable to change. It means co-ordinating efforts for change by whites and avoiding the haphazard, sporadic, guilt-salving gestures of the past. It means being cool-headed in assessing priorities and strategies. It means stretching the minds of white South Africans by presenting radical alternatives to the existing social order. In the long run, it means being available for negotiation in crisis situations from which change may result, and it means having accepted the implications of black leadership and offering to contribute skills, insights and resources to that leadership.

White consciousness recognises the importance of the role of writers, poets and artists in the processes of change. In the polarisation and confrontation that are increasingly going to characterise our society, true literature and art will continue to transcend any ideology, with personal integrity as their criterion. As interpreters who crystallise the issues and communicate their significance, artists have the very important function of relating to all those who themselves have integrity in relating to others irrespective of colour. Artists are able to interpret our situation and speak to people of all groups in a universal medium and in a way that academics, journalists and clergy cannot because they are so firmly labelled in their ethnic or denominational boxes *(53)*. This is one reason why Spro-cas 2 has published work by James Matthews, Gladys Thomas, Wopko Jensma, Nadine Gordimer and Andrè Brink.

Role of the Church

The Spro-cas Church Commission stated that 'the Church is still in a unique position to promote inter-racial contact, communication and dialogue on a large scale and should make effective use of its opportunities' *(54)*. In view of the importance of cross-cutting affiliations, already mentioned, and particularly since within the church all people should be able to meet on a basis of complete acceptance and equality, irrespective of colour or class, the church is potentially a major agency for social change. In order to be this, however, and to assist in the achievement of a more just social order 'it must organise its own life and government consistently with the Gospel of Jesus Christ' *(55)*. The Church Commission found in fact that the church reflects the basic patterns of discrimination and inequality of the broader society and 'an immediate and urgent aim must therefore be the removal of all forms of racialism from the institutional structure of the Church'.

Both the Spro-cas Church and Economics Commissions detailed a number of specific recommendations for the Churches to consider and, if possible, to implement. These included the better utilisation of church land in rural areas, the re-distribution of church finance in order to promote community development, a programme to educate church members with a view to making them well-informed and creative agents of social change, the refusal by churches to describe themselves in legal documents as white or African or Coloured for Group Areas purposes, and a reviewing of relationships with church schools which do not accept black children.

A number of relevant efforts have been embarked on in recent years, notably the Anglican Human Relations Programme, the programmes of the Wilgespruit Fellowship Centre, the work of the Catholic Justice and Peace Commissions and Spro-cas. The Christian Institute has recently formulated a series of theological statements and a programme of action, both directed at social change. The South African Council of Churches has invited its members to participate in a Justice and Reconciliation Division. Most of these programmes are slow to show significant results, largely because of the inertia of the churches themselves, and because of their cumbersome structures. There also seems generally to be lacking a sufficiently rigorous conceptual framework from which aims, objectives and strategies flow organically, so that much of the work has been irrelevant or spasmodic and haphazard.

I believe that Spro-cas is of significance as a model for change-oriented programmes, and that the following features, amongst others, are worthy of consideration:

(i)   Spro-cas has been a programme, or a series of inter-related programmes and projects. It is not an organisation.

(ii)   It has been temporary and short-term, with its own death envisaged from the start.

(iii) It has been a sustained and reasonably systematic effort (theology, study commissions, action programmes).

(iv)   Its structure has been very simple and flexible, and its work has not been hampered by a hierarchy of committees.

(v)   It has operated, in the action phase, through clearly demarcated black community programmes and white consciousness programmes. (This has in fact resulted in a very high degree of co-operation between black and white staff). The basic assumption underlying this structure was that a 'multi-racial' programme would not be able effectively to meet the different needs of blacks and whites.

(vi)   It has generated a number of spill-over effects which have been allowed to develop, or, if they have not proved relevant, to die.

(vii) It has been able to take risks and to risk failure. It has adopted tactics of confrontation when these seemed right.

(viii) It has set itself realistic objectives and has tried to clarify its strategies.

(ix) It has followed an action-reflection model.
(x)   It has, in the process of its work, accumulated skills and resources which
      can provide the basis for on-going activities.

While Spro-cas may be a useful model for programmes for social change, I
do not intend to suggest that it can be regarded as a model for the Church itself. One challenge to the Church, however, is the need to scrutinise its own
life style. 'There is urgent need for systematic assessment of the role of Christians and ecclesiastical institutions in supporting, wittingly or unwittingly,
the violence which often masquerades as 'order' in the contemporary world.
Awareness must be matched by actions which befit repentence' (56).

The traditional alliance between church and wealth is one example of the
problem, and another is the alliance between the church and the military,
'symbolised by military chaplaincies, regimental flags in churches, and
ambivalence towards conscientious objectors' (57). In this connection it is
significant that the State has given R1 500 000 for the activities of the various
churches in the armed forces. The Chaplain General is quoted as saying that
'Churches are provided with all the means to carry on their work according to
their customs and methods since the religious preparedness of the young man
is of utmost importance to the State in this time of threat. We cannot thank
God enough for a government which is aware of, and strives to fulfil, its
Christian calling' (58).

Viewed in the context of world Christendom's concern for the structural
violence and the injustice in our social system — the direct cause of the threat
mentioned — need more be said?

This report is being written in great haste, for a number of reasons, the most
immediate being the threat posed to the work of Spro-cas by the Commission
of Enquiry into Certain Organisations (the Schlebusch Commission). I am
anxious that the draft should be completed as soon as possible, and must thus
omit much that I had planned to include. I would have wished, for example, to
deal more adequately with the role of the church in bringing about social
change. Instead, it seems appropriate to conclude this section with the
following prophetic words from the report of the Spro-cas Social Commission:

the Church may have to intervene if there is a strong move towards
further totalitarianism. The lesson to be learned from Nazi Germany is
that the Church is the only effective institution for combating a totalitarian regime. The efforts of trade unions, newspapers, universities,
opposition parties are of little avail. Hitler succeeded against all of these
but never succeeded in 'breaking' the Church to his will.

Strategies for Change

Reforming the System

There are a number of valuable suggestions for action aimed at social change in the Spro-cas literature. The sets of recommendations in the reports of the Education, Economics and Church reports, for example, are strategies in themselves, taking their starting point as the reality of the present position and suggesting feasible actions which can be carried out within the existing social framework. The rationale behind such strategies is that 'although these changes will not themselves bring about the Responsible Society, they nevertheless will represent a movement towards it' *(59)*, and that work within the system should not be under-rated: 'if all South African Christians accept this limited number of recommendations and act upon them a significant leavening force in the South African social situation will have been created ... which will lead to still further changes' *(60)*. On the assumption that social change is an incremental process, positive steps such as those suggested by the Commissions can play an important role in the achievement of fundamental change, the major redistribution of power, wealth and land mentioned earlier in this report. The recommendations by the Commissions relate to such important matters as access to educational opportunity; the financing of education; improvements in educational facilities for blacks; a liberal approach to knowledge; the phasing out of migrant labour; the establishment of works committees, under certain conditions *(61)*, as a prelude to trade union rights for all; the creation of adult education and literacy schemes; eradication of inequalities in the taxation system; the elimination of prison labour; the equalisation of stipends paid to clergy; the creation of additional bursary and scholarship funds by the Churches; the encouragement of ecumenical communities, and a re-examination by the Churches of their investment policies *(62)*. This list is merely a selection from almost 100 specific recommendations made by these three Commissions. The recommendations as a whole obviously provide a unique opportunity for Churches and other agencies to formulate systematic programmes for reform in South Africa. Unfortunately, there is as yet little evidence that they are being viewed in this light, and church-initiated programmes in particular seem too often to fall back on the easier options of study and dissemination of factual information.

Migrant Labour

Strategies in specific fields are suggested at other places in the Spro-cas literature. The report on migrant labour by Dr Francis Wilson, for example, contains an extremely thoughtful formula for the phasing out of migrant labour *(63)*, starting with an acceptance of the fact of urbanisation among

Africans and following through the practical implications that follow from this. Dr Wilson sees the problem as being a choice facing white South Africans: 'So long as the economy continues to grow, urbanisation will continue to take place. Whites still have the opportunity to take steps to ease this socio-economic transition for the welfare of all. But unless action is taken now ... the consequences of the migrant system will ravage South Africa' *(64)*. The practical steps envisaged by Dr Wilson include the provision of freehold tenure for all those with rights to be in town, the repeal of the Bantu Labour Regulations of 1968, the setting of a target date for the elimination of the pass laws by amending the Urban Areas Act, and a crash programme for building family accommodation in the urban areas. All the churches, including the NG Kerk, are deeply concerned about the evils of the migrant labour system *(65)*, there have recently been indications that the government is being forced to accept the fact of permanent urbanisation of Africans in 'white' areas *(66)*, and the Deputy Minister of Bantu Administration has called for assistance in re-thinking the pass laws *(67)*. All these things suggest that the time is right for a concerted drive aimed at the phasing out of migrant labour, and Dr Wilson's formula is an extremely valuable tool for this.

Management Responsibility

Another specific field is the role of white employers and management. Sprocas 2 has made a number of proposals in this regard, including the establishment of a code of employment practices, embracing not only wages, but also social security of workers, effective consultation with workers, and training and productivity *(68)*. Dr Rick Turner has dealt challengingly with the concepts of worker participation and worker control in *The Eye of the Needle*, published by Spro-cas 2 in 1972. (Since Dr Turner has been banned by the South African government under the 'Suppression of Communism' Act, he cannot be quoted).

A useful code of management responsibilities is contained in the report of a panel, under the convenorship of Dr Beyers Naudè, which investigated the Palabora Mining Company *(69)*. This code deals with general policy, wages and fringe benefits, job advancement and training, labour organisation and labour relations, social relations and contributions towards general development, and provides a lucid and comprehensive yardstick whereby the performances of employers can be measured in terms of their moral responsibility in an exploitative economic system which disadvantages black workers. Companies wishing to assess their own role, and pressure groups outside the companies, will both find the code a useful tool.

The Police

A third specific field is dealt with by Professor Barend van Niekerk who lists ten recommendations for improvements in the role of the police, which he suggests that public institutions, notably the press, should stress at every opportunity *(70)*. These recommendations include improvement in the salaries of all policemen and the elimination of racial discrimination in salary scales, more advancement possibilities for black policemen, improved police protection in black townships, the gradual phasing out of influx control measures which lead to arrests of many Africans, less overt identification by high-ranking police officers with the interests of the party in power, and a complete ban on the making of political statements by such officers. Professor van Niekerk adds that recommendations regarding the security police system would be so radical as not to be worth making at present, but that the public and its institutions, 'in order to prepare the avenues of change', should maintain and step up 'their vigilance over the use and abuse of our security legislation'.

Towards Social Change

The report of the Spro-cas Social Commission contains a number of very valuable individual contributions which should be seriously considered by all those working for change in South Africa. Dr M.G. Whisson, for example, analyses the potentials for change afforded by the social institutions, including the press, the churches, the voluntary associations, occupational groupings, and the (white) political parties. With regard to the latter, his conclusion bears out the analysis contained earlier in this report on the role of the entire white political system: 'By the education, conversion or coercion of the electorate a climate of opinion (values, aspirations and fears) must be created within which the policies of *all* the parties will be compelled to change ...' *(71)*. This is more likely to be productive than working from within any of the parties.

In the same report Mr L. Douwes Dekker suggests a programme of change through the institutional network, including systematic coverage and publicity regarding decisions taken by organisations concerned with the 'hidden association', so that these can be scrutinised, and the creation of an ombudsman organisation in the field of institutional relations *(72)*. Professor H. Lever proposes a programme to reduce inter-group tensions which includes educational programmes to combat prejudice, the use of propaganda and research *(73)*.

Spro-cas 2 has been profoundly influenced by the chapter on 'Strategies for Change' by Professor L. Schlemmer in the report of the Spro-cas Social Commission. Professor Schlemmer's analysis of the potential forces for change, his assessment of meaningful change and his recommendations regarding strategic action directed towards whites have underlain much of the work we have attempted to undertake *(74)*. His chapter also includes a section on strategic action directed towards blacks, which contains many challenging and valuable insights. A brief summary could not do justice to Professor Schlemmer's thinking, and I can only say that I regard it as essential reading for those working for change in South Africa. What is worth reproducing here is Professor Schlemmer's list of criteria as to what constitutes meaningful change in the present situation. This list provides a useful yardstick against which to measure priorities and strategies.

The type of change which is desirable in South Africa is that which will:

(i) lead to steady improvements in the economic position of the majority of blacks, and

(ii) have the effect of closing the gap in average standards of living between black and white groups;

(iii) result in steady improvements in regard to the civil liberties, social benefits, and freedom under the law enjoyed by members of all groups in the population of South Africa;

(iv) lead to a political arrangement in South Africa which will avoid the exploitation and control of any one group by another group;

(v) allow all members of all groups to enjoy self-esteem, pride, dignity and a release from those factors which presently undermine the morale and self-respect of individual members of black groups, as well as an elimination of factors which undermine the social 'health' of whole communities, particularly the poorer ones.

A Model for Transition

One of the early expectations of the sponsors of Spro-cas was that the project would provide an 'alternative to apartheid' which could be effectively sold to the white electorate. The work of the commissions, particularly the Social and Political Commissions, has indicated clearly that this can be no facile exercise of proposing, for example, a common roll with either a qualified franchise or universal franchise. Nor can it be some tidy scheme for partition or enlightened 'separate development'.

The Political Commission has made a major contribution to South African political thinking through its rigorous analysis of the real issues at stake and its stripping away of the flabby thinking surrounding such concepts as 'integration', 'apartheid', 'the common society', and the 'plural states approach'. It has also provided a profound critique of the Westminster model in the South African setting, and, indeed, of the whole liberal-constitutional approach. Recognising the importance of the groups in our society it has presented a formula for transition in the direction of such ethical principles as effective participation in government and the safeguarding of personal and civil rights. This formula is aimed at the creation of an 'open pluralist' society in place of the present apartheid one, and as a more realistic alternative than the perhaps mythical 'common society'. Tested against the Commission's own criteria of ethical acceptability and practical feasibility, the formula or model for transition arises logically from a rigorous analysis of the potentials for change in the present political situation. Mr A.B. du Toit of Stellenbosch University was largely responsible for this whole section (Part 3 and Part 4) of the report.

The model for transition can perhaps be viewed as the last opportunity presented to white South Africa to make meaningful adjustments and accommodations before the major initiative is finally wrested from their hands. The model follows a multiple strategy approach which 'seeks to make a variety of distinctions, for example between change within the framework of the present political system and change outside that framework', recognising that different sectors of society can contribute to change in different ways. The model involves two stages, which are not proposed as a rigid chronological scheme, so that work to realise the second stage can be engaged upon immediately. If both stages were to be completed, there would have been a major devolution of power, with the creation of an open pluralist society and the basic structure of a new political system embodying a federal, multi-racial government. The specific recommendations are contained in the final chapter of the Spro-cas Political Report. There are indications that thinking people in the white political parties and in extra-parliamentary initiatives like *Verligte Aksie* are taking a serious look at the proposals, although it is still too early (the Political Report was published in June 1973) to say to what extent they will be influenced in practical terms.

FOOTNOTES

1. *South Africa's Political Alternatives,* report of the Spro-cas Political Commission, p. 42. See also Peter Walshe: *African Nationalism in South Africa,* forthcoming from Spro-cas/Ravan Press. Prof. Walshe points out that by the early 1900s sixteen percent of the common roll in the Cape was made up of black voters and that this offered the vision of a steadily expanding participation by blacks in the political system. This vision was, of course, shattered by the Act of Union.
2. Nimrod Mkele: 'Domesticating the African', unpublished paper, 1959, p. 19.
3. See, for example, Bennie Khoapa: 'The New Black' and Njabulo Ndebele: 'Black Development' in *Black Viewpoint,* Spro-cas Black Community Programs, 1972; SASO Policy Manifesto, quoted in *Black Review,* BCP, 1973, pp. 40-44; N.C. Manganyi: *Being-Black-in-the-World,* Spro-cas, 1973; Ben Langa (ed.): *Creativity and Black Development,* SASO, 1973 (now banned). Also, for example, report of the first national congress of the Black People's Convention, December, 1972.

4. B. Khoapa, op. cit., p. 64.
5. Ibid., p. 67.
6. See *Handbook of Black Organisations,* BCP, 1973.
7. Details of these and other organisations are given in *Handbook,* op. cit., and *Black Review,* op. cit.
8. Ross Snyder: article in *The Christian Century,* 3 April, 1973.
9. N.C. Manganyi: *Black Consciousness and the Buthelezi Dilemma,* forthcoming from Spro-cas/Ravan.
10. James Matthews: 'Dialogue' in *Cry Rage!,* Spro-cas 1972 (this volume is now banned).
11. *Black Review,* op. cit., p. 77.
12. N.C. Manganyi: op. cit.
13. Report of the first national congress of the Black Peoples Convention, December, 1972, pp. 5-8.
14. F. van Zyl Slabbert: 'Cultural and Ethnic Politics' in *Towards Social Change,* report of the Spro-cas Social Commission, pp. 70-71.
15. *Towards Social Change,* op. cit., p. 49.
16. *Towards Social Change,* op. cit., p. 16.
17. Ibid., p. 49.
18. See 'The Political System', Chapter 3.
19. *Rand Daily Mail,* 25 July, 1973.
20. *Rand Daily Mail,* 25 July 1973, p. 1.
21. Ibid.
22. M.G. Whisson: 'Organisations available for Change' in *Towards Social Change,* op. cit., p. 94.
23. Ibid., p. 95.
24. Fatima Meer: 'The Indian People' in *South Africa's Minorities,* Spro-cas Occasional Publication 2, 1971, p. 30.
25. van Zyl Slabbert, op. cit., p. 63.
26. In recent weeks, the press has carried warnings of potential racial tension and conflict by Mr Sonny Leon, Chief Buthelezi, Dr Beyers Naudé, and Mr Theo Gerdener. amongst others. See, for example: 'Southern Africa faces race war — Spro-cas report', *Cape Times* 8 June 1973; 'Reform or face War — Naudé, *Rand Daily Mail,* 13 June 1973: 'Schools, not guns, wanted — Randall', *Rand Daily Mail,* 22 June 1973; 'Close gap or face revolt — Buthelezi', *Rand Daily Mail,* 25 July 1973.
27. L. Schlemmer: 'Strategies for Change' in *Towards Social Change,* op. cit., p. 161.
28. Ibid.
29. Ibid.
30. *South Africa's Political Alternatives,* op. cit., p. 151.
31. Editorial, *Die Transvaler,* 24 July 1973.
32. See *Power, Privilege and Poverty,* report of the Spro-cas Economics Commission, Chapter 6; *Towards Social Change,* op. cit., p. 19, p. 160, pp. 107-108; *South Africa's Political Alternatives,* op. cit., p. 50 et seq.
33. *Power, Privilege and Poverty,* op. cit., p. 22.
34. Ibid., p. 69.
35. Ibid., p. 68.
36. For some details see *Power, Privilege and Poverty,* Chapter 6.
37. Survey by the South African Institute of Race Relations, reported in *Rand Daily Mail,* 18 July 1973.
38. See, for example, L. Schlemmer: *The Negro Ghetto Riots and South African Cities,* Topical Talk 15, SAIRR, 1968.

39. There is considerable evidence that black consumers are discriminated against, although they pay as much as whites. For example, *Business Times* (11 Feb., 1973) reported that a large Johannesburg discount store, Frymer-Moshal, offers free life insurance policies of R10 000 for a month to white customers who buy R40 or more worth of goods at a time. Blacks who buy the same amount receive policies for only R5 000. The reason given was that blacks have a higher mortality rate than whites. This example illustrates in a rather macabre manner how the vicious cycle of inequality is perpetuated.
40. *Rand Daily Mail*, 25 July 1973.
41. *South Africa's Political Alternatives*, op. cit., p. 46.
42. *Power, Privilege and Poverty*, op. cit., p. 55.
43. H. Adam: *Modernising Racial Domination*, University of California Press, 1971, p. 153.
44. L. Schlemmer: 'Strategies for Change', op. cit., p. 174.
45. H. Adam, op. cit., p. 155.
46. Peter Walshe, op. cit. (footnote 1), gives a brief history of the ICU and its interaction with African political movements of the period.
47. *Black Review*, op. cit., p. 45. (The same publication describes some of the actions taken by black workers during 1972, p. 114ff.).
48. Leo Kuper, quoted in *South Africa's Political Alternatives*, op. cit., p. 85.
49. H. Lever: 'Practical Programme to Reduce Inter-Group Tension' in *Towards Social Change*, op. cit., p. 140.
50. See *South Africa's Political Alternatives*, op. cit., comments on the 'common society', e.g. p. 73.
51. L. Douwes Dekker: 'Change through the Institutional Network' in *Towards Social Change*, op. cit., p. 111ff.
52. See, for example, H. Kleinschmidt (ed.): *White Liberation*, Spro-cas 2, 1973.
53. See, for example, the views of Mrs Fatima Meer, president of the Association for Sociology in Southern Africa, on 'white sociology' and 'white anthropology': *The Star*, 12 July 1973 (feature article by Patrick Laurence).
54. *Apartheid and the Church*, report of the Spro-cas Church Commission, p. 71.
55. Ibid.
56. World Council of Churches: Report of the Consultation on Violence, Non-Violence and the Struggle for Social Justice, Cardiff 1972, p. 25.
57. Ibid.
58. *Ecunews*, 23 July 1973, p. 3.
59. *Power, Privilege and Poverty*, op. cit., p. 104.
60. *Education Beyond Apartheid*, report of the Spro-cas Education Commission, p. 59-61.
61. That a national body of works committees be established, in order that experience may be shared and direction given; that works committees should have access to relevant Industrial Councils or Wages Boards; that members elected to serve on Works Committees should be given specific training regarding their role as representatives of the workers: *Power, Privilege and Poverty*, op. cit., p. 106.
62. *Education Beyond Apartheid*: Chapter 7; *Power, Privilege and Poverty*: Chapter 9; *Apartheid and the Church*: Chapter 4.
63. F. Wilson: *Migrant Labour in South Africa*, Spro-cas/SACC, 1972, p. 213ff.
64. Ibid., p. 217-218.
65. Ibid., see Appendix (vi), 'Church Statements on Migrant Labour'.
66. See *Rapport*, 5 August 1973.
67. See *Sunday Tribune*, 5 August 1973, p. 1.

68. See release by Spro-cas Labour Panel in Part 2 of this report.
69. *Management Responsibility and African Employment:* published by Ravan Press and distributed by Spro-cas, 1973, p. 59.
70. *Law, Justice and Society,* report of the Spro-cas Legal Commission, pp. 63-64.
71. *Towards Social Change,* op. cit., p. 77.
72. Ibid., p. 126, et seq.
73. Ibid., p. 136, et seq.
74. Ibid., p. 156, et seq.

The world has arrived at a point where Utopia alone is realistic

André Bieler: *Calvin, prophet of the Industrial Era*

Chapter Five

THE NEW SOCIETY

THERE IS clearly a need to think beyond the immediate and urgent problem of racial inequality in South Africa towards a freer, more fulfilling and creative social order. As Professor Schlemmer says, 'Even the most prosperous, privileged and self-satisfied whites live in a state of unfreedom which compels them to conform to a pattern of existence in which status and success are the gods, and which is becoming increasingly associated with mindless mass-consumption, nervous diseases, congestion, pollution and bureaucracy' (1). All of us are denied the opportunity to achieve our full humanity, to pursue without restriction 'the development of expressive artistic and creative abilities, an openness to the rewards of warm and empathic contact with others, an acceptance of different points of view and ways of living, and the notion that human beings are free to change and recreate their social life' (2). In our formative years we are taught, both directly and indirectly, such basic values as competitiveness, materialism and an unquestioning group-identification. These values inevitably shape the structure of our society.

In a situation where we are not able to be whole men, where our spiritual and intellectual capacities are stunted and twisted, where we live daily with a system of overt and institutionalised violence, the Church has a particular calling to be involved in the struggle to make all things new. Christian love must resist all that humiliates man, all that restricts his freedom, all that oppresses or exploits him, and all that alienates him from his fellows (3).

When reading the Gospel narrative one clearly sees the deep concern Christ had for life on all levels. Christ is concerned about people who suffer from physical disability (sickness, cripples), economic deprivation (the poor), restrictions on their freedom (those in prison), alienation from society (lepers, mentally disturbed and prostitutes). While the Gospels focus on the situation of the individual and how his plight can be relieved, sociology, economics and political science now give us insight into the forces that shape our society. It would be plainly irresponsible today if we still confined our concern to providing relief for the individual, rather than changing those forces and structures in society which cause deprivation and suffering (4).

What then have these disciplines to say about the form of the society towards which we should work?

Education

There should be equality of educational opportunity. This means that every person in society should have equal access to the best education that the state can provide and have available an education which is best suited to his age, ability and aptitude *(5)*.

The long-term goals of an equitable education system can be expressed as follows *(6):*

(i) Primary education shall be compulsory for all children, and shall be free. Where schools, for geographical reasons, are racially homogeneous, education authorities and teachers shall ensure that children of different racial groups meet in social, cultural and sporting contacts.

(ii) Secondary education shall be equally available to all on merit, and shall be free to the same age limit for all pupils. Such education shall be of equivalent quality wherever it is provided and shall include vocational, technical and commercial high schools open to all pupils educationally qualified to enter them.

(iii) Teacher training shall, as far as possible, be conducted in colleges and universities open to all qualified educationally to enter them, and shall be of equivalent standard. Special attention shall be given to instructing teacher trainees in the promotion of inter-group tolerance and understanding in schools. There shall be no discrimination on the grounds of race in the salaries or conditions of service of teachers.

(iv) University education of the highest quality available in South Africa shall be accessible equally to all persons qualified by academic criteria to receive it.

In his book, *The Eye of the Needle,* Dr Rick Turner has dealt challengingly with the concept of education for freedom and has suggested ways in which education should be structured, other than according to the traditional Western model. As Dr Turner has been banned I regretfully cannot quote his views here.

The Economic System

The Spro-cas Economics Commission based its long-term goals on the concept of the Responsible Society, as defined by Dr W.A. Visser t'Hooft:

> A Responsible Society is a society in which all members have the opportunity to share fully in the common responsibility for the decisions affecting the common life. The universal demand for emancipation and participation which has found such an explosive manifestation in our time is fundamentally the demand of men to be treated as human beings and has its roots in the Judaeo-Christian tradition as well as in the other main conceptions of life which have created our civilisation. The ethic of the Responsible Society must take its stand against all philosophies or practices in the life of the state or of industry which treat adult men as objects rather than subjects *(7)*.

The Commission felt that a Responsible Society would contain the following positive economic principles *(8)*:

(i)   Development exists for man, not man for development: the process of development must serve to enhance the dignity of all in the society. The manipulation and exploitation of some for the benefit of the privileged have no place in the Responsible Society.

(ii)   The goal must not simply be economic growth: the ultimate goal of development should be social justice. Economic growth by itself is not enough: South Africa has been one of the most rapidly developing countries, yet the lion's share of the increased wealth has gone to only a few, whilst in some sectors the majority have actually grown poorer.

(iii)   There must not be poverty in the midst of plenty.

(iv)   Power should be shared: every worker should have a voice in the conduct of business or industry which is carried on by means of his labour. It is immoral to structure society so that those who put money into an enterprise have a say in its running, but not those who put their selves, their sweat and toil into it. (The Commission recognised the difficulty of the problem of how society should be ordered to achieve this end: some argue for nationalisation of the economy, so making it subject to the will of the people; others fear the possible resulting concentration of political and economic power in the same hands. But, the Commission concludes, it is of fundamental importance that Christians become fully aware of the structure of power in the society so that they may participate creatively in a discussion on the ways in which power may be distributed *(9))*.

(v)   Risks should be shared: if capitalists should receive a premium for investing their money in a particularly risky enterprise, this should hold true too for workers.

(vi)   There should be equality of opportunity in education and in all spheres of economic activity. Under this principle job reservation, discriminatory entrepreneurial opportunities and inequality in the ownership of the means of production stand condemned.

The models offered by African socialism in Tanzania, as expressed in the writings of Julius Nyerere, and certain European countries are relevant in any consideration of a future South Africa. One of the hopeful factors is that the options of homeland and other black leaders are not yet closed and they have opportunities for experimentation, perhaps along the lines of the Tanzanian Ujamaa village schemes.

I would again have wished here to quote the views of Dr R. Turner on the politics of socialism and such concepts as workers' control, and on the measures which are possible to counteract tendencies towards an oligarchic concentration of power.

The Law

From the primary Christian ethical concepts of equality, freedom, love, brotherhood, responsibility and the use of ethical means, it is possible to derive such concepts as the Rule of Law and guaranteed civil rights.

The Spro-cas Commissions attach particular emphasis to the need for a restoration of the Rule of Law in South Africa. As an institution, the Rule of Law *(10)*:

(i)   serves to limit arbitrary governmental power and to diminish the possibility of the abuse of political authority;

(ii)   helps to ensure that conflict situations, especially those between the citizen and the state, will be dealt with in a fair and rational way;

(iii)   leads to certainty and predictability, and therefore to a more rational ordering of affairs, in the area of its operation;

(iv)   when operating effectively, it gives to the citizen the assurance that disputes with others, including the government, will be resolved justly according to fair procedures. This feeling that disputes will be justly resolved contributes to security and loyalty in the state.

The principles underlying the Rule of Law are (11)

(iv)   that the citizen's right to freedom of the person, expression and association, subject to traditional and narrowly defined limitations (such as the laws governing defamation and treason), shall be honoured by the state;

(ii)   that governmental action affecting such rights shall be authorised only in terms of general laws which prescribe specific standards for interference with, or limitation of, such rights;

(iii)   that adjudication over such rights, and permissible interferences with them, shall be in the hands of impartial tribunals (preferably the ordinary courts) which shall act according to fair trial procedures (or due process of law).

An important aspect of the Rule of Law is thus the citizen's right to have a hearing before an impartial and independent tribunal when he alleges an unjustified interference with his constitutional safeguards. The Spro-cas Political Report describes the manner in which the Rule of Law must be realised through the legislature (which must not invade the fundamental liberties of the citizen, except for limited periods during emergencies), the executive (which must itself be subject to law in that its actions are limited and controlled by specific provisions of law), the judiciary (which must be independent and act according to fair trial procedures), and the criminal law (which must have certainty in the definition of crimes and must not be retrospective) (12).

The Rule of Law is thus very largely concerned with the protection of the individual freedoms of the person, of speech, movement and association. Such rights should be guaranteed in a written constitution and enforced by independent courts, although one recognises that constitutionally protected civil rights can be trampled underfoot by the State and that without the necessary social foundations constitutional enactment will be inadequate to secure recognition of the basic civil liberties *(13)*. Nevertheless the guarantee of civil rights 'is a goal to be striven towards, and the incorporation of such rights in a constitutional instrument may at least have an educative value in the community'.

The Political System

All the governed must have the opportunity to participate effectively in government at *all* levels. The political system must 'allow individual freedom of both opportunity and affiliation as well as giving scope for social and cultural diversity' *(14)*.

Two principles should underlie the ordering of society: no citizen or group may be denied representation in and effective access to the highest legislative and executive authorities, and local and communal institutions must have effective powers and resources, as well as being adapted to the specific needs and claims of individuals and groups *(15)*.

Government power should not be used to enforce a centrally determined policy in inter-personal social relations, cultural and educational affairs. There must be the highest possible degree of freedom of action 'for all kinds of voluntary associations and secondary groups such as professional groups, trade unions, business groups, cultural groups, churches and universities to manage their own affairs within bounds fixed by law' *(16)*. Pluralism of this nature is 'a necessary counterweight to the power of government and as a necessary base for a free society' *(17)*. In a large, heterogeneous society such as ours these ideals may best be furthered through a federal structure, proportional representation, and large measures of regional or communal autonomy, which will help to separate and distribute the power of government.

In broad and necessarily general terms this appears to be the basic consensus to have emerged from the six Spro-cas study commissions. The challenge before white South Africans is to decide whether this is, in fact, the future society they wish to bring about, and, if so, to face up to the implications of working towards it, approaching this 'in the light of Sartre's distinction between a *gesture* and an *act*. An act implies involvement, with the whole chain of cause and effect, it leads to something, it has a direct moral bearing on the situation in which it is performed' *(18)*. The challenge before black South Africans is to measure this vision against their own aspirations and if necessary to propose alternatives, and using their rapidly developing initiative, to promote these. We are at a delicately poised turning point in our history and the decisions to be taken by both black and white in the near future will profoundly influence the shape of the society to come.

FOOTNOTES

1. L. Schlemmer: 'Strategies for Change' in *Towards Social Change,* report of the Spro-cas Social Commission, p. 191.
2. *Towards Social Change,* op. cit., p. 50.
3. *Spro-cas: Five Biblical Principles* (Danie van Zyl, 1972).
4. Ibid.
5. *Education Beyond Apartheid,* report of the Spro-cas Education Commission, p. 9.
6. Ibid., p. 58.
7. *Power, Privilege and Poverty,* report of the Spro-cas Economics Commission, p. 9, where the full definition is given.
8. Ibid., pp. 11-15.
9. There is little overt propagation of socialist alternatives in South Africa, partly because of the confusion and fear surrounding that term amongst whites. One recent effort has been *Katatura,* Aug.-Sept., 1973, the publication of the National Catholic Federation of Students (South Africa).
10. *South Africa's Political Alternatives,* report of the Spro-cas Political Commission, p. 14.
11. Ibid., pp. 15-16.
12. Ibid., pp. 16-17.
13. Ibid., pp. 17-18, and D.B. Molteno in *Law, Justice and Society,* report of the Spro-cas Legal Commission, p. 90ff.
14. *South Africa's Political Alternatives,* op. cit., p. 215.
15. Ibid.
16. Ibid., p. 217.
17. Ibid.
18. André Brink: *Spro-cas Background Paper 8.*

PART TWO

REPORT ON SPROCAS

REPORT ON SPRO-CAS

CONTENTS

1   Spro-cas : Chronology of Events

NOTE: This is an attempt to list only those events which the Spro-cas staff regard as particularly significant. There have been a host of seminars, conferences and addresses which are not indicated here.

SACC = South African Council of Churches
CI   = Christian Institute of Southern Africa
BCP   = Black Community Programmes

1968

September: Publication of *The Message to the People of South Africa* by the Theological Commission of the SACC.

1969

February: Decision by the CI and the SACC to establish a study porject to follow up the *Message*.

March: Appointment of Peter Randall as director of Spro-cas.

August: First meeting of Spro-cas Social Commission at Koinonia, Botha's Hill.
First meeting of Spro-cas Church Commission in Johannesburg.
First meeting of Spro-cas Education Commission in Johannesburg.
First meeting of Spro-cas Political Commission at Schonstatt, Cape Town.

September: First meeting of Spro-cas Economics Commission in Johannesburg.

1970

February: Interim Statement by Spro-cas Education Commission
                 Interim Statement by Spro-cas Political Commission

May: First meeting of Spro-cas Legal Commission in
                 Johannesburg.
                 Publication by SACC of *The Church and the Death Penalty*
                 by Peter Randall.

December: Publication of *Anatomy of Apartheid*, Spro-cas Occasional
                 Publication No. 1.

1971

January: Publication of *South Africa's Minorities*, Spro-cas
                 Occasional Publication No. 2.

February: Publication of *Directions of Change in S.A. Politics*, Spro-
                 cas Occasional Publication No. 3.
                 Spro-cas participation in Umtata Theological Workshop.

March: Interim Statement by Spro-cas Education Commission
                 Paper on Federalism by Japie Basson released (*Rand Daily
                 Mail* 1/3/71).

April: Publication of *Some Implications of Inequality*, Spro-cas
                 Occasional Publication No. 4.

May: Decision by CI to sponsor Spro-cas 2. Spro-cas papers
                 presented and discussed at *Platform* meetings, University
                 of Natal. Paper on The Police Force by Prof. B. van Niekerk
                 released (*RDM* 6/5/71).

June: Address by Peter Randall to annual conference of S.A.
                 Indian Teachers' Association, Durban.

August: Address by Peter Randall to SACC National Conference,
                 Durban.
                 Decision by SACC to sponsor Spro-cas 2.
                 Publication of *Education beyond Apartheid*, report of the
                 Spro-cas Education Commission.
                 Spro-cas participation in Consultation on Social Change,
                 Wilgespruit.

November: Planning meeting for Spro-cas 2 under chairmanship of
                 Archbishop Hurley.

December: Publication of *Towards Social Change*, report of the Spro-
                 cas Social Commission.

1972

January: Spro-cas 2 offices established in Johannesburg, Cape Town
                 and Durban.
                 Bennie Khoapa appointed director of Spro-cas Black Com-
                 munity Programmes.
                 Rev Danie van Zyl appointed Spro-cas Communications
                 Director.
                 Neville Curtis appointed Spro-cas Organiser in Cape Town.
                 Memorandum on reactions to Spro-cas Education Report
                 issued (*Star* 10/1/72).
                 Spro-cas memorandum submitted to Select Committee on
                 the Health Bill.

February: Spro-cas workshop at annual conference of Swiss Mission,
                 Valdezia.

March: Spro-cas/CI memorandum presented to delegation from
                 International Metalworkers' Federation.

April: Horst Kleinschmidt appointed Spro-cas white conscious-
                 ness programme organiser, Johannesburg.

May: BCP Conference for Black Church Leaders, Edendale.
                 Spro-cas participation in seminar of Labour Party Youth,
                 Johannesburg.
                 Publication of *The Eye of the Needle*, by Dr R. Turner.
                 Education Campaign at Wits., Address by Horst Klein-
                 schmidt.

June: Publication of *Power, Privilege and Poverty*, report of the
                 Spro-cas Economics Commission.
                 Publication of first Spro-cas Background Paper.
                 Spro-cas participation in Witwatersrand Christian Council
                 meeting on student protest.
                 BCP Workshop on Community Development, Edendale.

Spro-cas participation in conference of high school scholars, Cape Town.

Address by Bennie Khoapa at University of Cape Town.

July: Spro-cas participation in Seminar on Education for Social Justice. Archdiocese of Durban Justice and Peace Commission

Spro-cas participation in Family Life Campaign in Johannesburg and Cape Town.

Seminar on Education and Society, arranged by Spro-cas and National Youth Action, Cape Town.

Celebration Mass for banned people, Johannesburg.

Ecumenical Protest Rally, Rondebosch Common.

Publication of first Spro-cas poster.

Steve Biko appointed BCP field worker, Durban.

Peter Randall awarded Christian Fellowship Trust travel grant.

Peter Randall's passport confiscated.

Spro-cas participation in Schools Conference, Durban.

August: Publication of *Apartheid and the Church*, report of the Spro-cas Church Commission.

Justice and Peace meetings in Durban and Pietermaritzburg addressed by Peter Randall and Danie van Zyl.

Spro-cas participation in regional meetings of Anglican Human Relations Programme, Elgin, Kwa Nzimela, Johannesburg, Modderpoort, Port Elizabeth.

BCP Follow-up Conference of Black Church Leaders, Edendale.

BCP Youth Leadership Conference, Edendale.

Spro-cas campaign for Code of Employment Practices.

September: Publication of *Black Viewpoint* by BCP (ed. S. Biko).

Bokwe Mafuna appointed BCP field worker, Johannesburg.

Publication of Spro-cas Biblical Principles (by Danie van Zyl).

October: Black Workers' Project established by BCP and SASO.

Spro-cas survey of church school domestic wages.

November: Statement by Spro-cas Labour Panel (*RDM* 6/11/72, *Cape Times* 7/11/72).

Publication of first Spro-cas dossier (on Namibia).

Publication of *Law, Justice and Society*, report of the Spro-cas Legal Commission.
Spro-cas participation in NUSAS Congress, Grahamstown.
Spro-cas strategy seminar, Stellenbosch.

December: Publication of *Cry Rage*, poems by James Matthews and Gladys Thomas.
Release of dossier on Labour Relations.
Resignation of Neville Curtis from Spro-cas staff.
Nikki Westcott appointed to Spro-cas Cape Town office.

1973

January: Spro-cas participation in Pilgrimage for Family Life.
Ravan Press (Pty.) Ltd. established.
Joint publication by Spro-cas and SACC of *Migrant Labour in South Africa* by Dr Francis Wilson.

February: Spro-cas series of public lectures on the Need for Reform, Johannesburg.
Spro-cas participation in Conference on Domestic Employment, Durban Catholic Archdiocese.
Address by Peter Randall to FELCSA Conference, Johannesburg.
Publication of first *Contact* communication.

March: Publication of *White Liberation* (ed. H. Kleinschmidt).
Banning of Bokwe Mafuna and Steve Biko.
Banning of *The Eye of the Needle*.
Banning of *Cry Rage*.
Spro-cas domestic wages collation released.
Publication of first Spro-cas Discussion Paper.
Publication of Strike dossier.
Seminar on School and Society, Cape Town.
BCP decision to establish autonomous body.
Spro-cas proposal for white Programme for Social Change.
Publication of *Black Review* by BCP (ed. B. Khoapa).

April: Horst Kleinschmidt's passport confiscated.
Refusal to return Peter Randall's passport.
Publication of Open Letter to Minister of Interior (*Sunday*

Tribune, 13/5/73, *Pro Veritate,* June 1973).
Resignation by Spro-cas staff from S.A. Institute of Race Relations
Publication of *Fear or Freedom.*
National tour by Spro-cas staff to discuss Programme for Social Change.

May-June: Spro-cas series of public lectures on The Need for Reform, Durban.

May: Publication of *Sing for our Execution* by Wopko Jensma (Ophir/Ravan).

June: Publication of *South Africa's Political Alternatives,* report of the Spro-cas Political Commission.
Spro-cas High School Winter School, Cape Town.
Publication of *Ophir 17* (Ophir/Ravan).
Inaugural Helen Suzman Lecture on Equality in Education at the Johannesburg College of Education given by Peter Randall.
Publication of *Management Responsibility and African Employment* (Ravan).
Publication of dossier on Black Student Dissent.

July: Spro-cas participation in Seminar on Development, Catholic Commission for Peace and Justice (Tvl.).
Spro-cas symposium at Theological Winter School, Catholic Archdiocese of Durban.
Opening address to NUSWEL Conference by Horst Kleinschmidt.
Spro-cas participation in Student Social Workers Conference, Johannesburg.

August: Spro-cas series of public lectures on The Need for Reform, Cape Town.
Spro-cas staff refuse to testify before Schlebusch Commission

NOTE: 'Spro-cas participation' in events generally refers to assistance in planning and/or organising, providing resource material (study kits, background papers, photographic displays etc), providing speakers and/or consultants, and assisting in follow-up activities. This has been one of the most creative and rewarding functions of Spro-cas staff and has often had significant results within the organisations and groups concerned, particularly in terms of re-thinking priorities and strategies.

It is partly the experience and insight gained in this kind of work that resulted in the Spro-cas proposals for a Programme for Social Change.

2. Membership of the Spro-cas Study Commissions

NOTE: All those who originally participated as members and consultants are listed. Not all of these actually signed the reports of their respective commissions. The signatories are listed in each report.

Spro-cas Church Commission

Dr D.W. Bandey
Rev D. Bax
Rt Rev B.B. Burnett (chairman)
Rev Dr C.W. Cook
Rev J.D. Davies
Rev J.W. de Gruchy (secretary)
Rev R. Ellis
Dr B. Engelbrecht
Rev T.S.N. Gqubule
Pastor D.J. Gqweta
Rev G. Hawkes
Prof B. Johanson
Very Rev J. Knutson
Rev Theo Kotze
Mr R. Legg
Rev D. Modisipodi
Ds C.F.B. Naudé
Very Rev P. Sandner
Rev A.D. Scholten
Rev Jerome Smith
Dr Elfie Strassberger
Rev J. Tau
Rev D. Tutu
Rev D. van Zyl
Mr A.C. Viljoen
Rev S.F. Windisch

Consultants

Prof A.S. Geyser
Rev R. Orr
Prof A.S. van Selms

Spro-cas Economics Commission

Mr R. Altman
Mr S. Archer
Dr E.A. Barker (chairman)
Dr R.T. Bell
Mr E.P. Bradlow
Mr M. Collier
Mr L. Douwes Dekker
Mr M. Fransman
Mr P. Goller
Mr D.C. Grice
Mr I.S. Haggie
Dr G.F. Jacobs M.P.
Mr R.U. Kenney
Mr H.C. Koch
Mr D. Lowry
Dr A.L. Müller
Prof S.B. Ngcobo
Dr R. Turner
Prof S.T. van der Horst
Dr F. Wilson (secretary)

Spro-cas Education Commission

Mr M.J. Ashley
Mr F.E. Auerbach
Mr C.H. Brigish
Mr O. Britzius
Mr C.B. Collins
Mr M. de Lisle
Prof A.P. Hunter
Rev A. Jennings
Sir Richard Luyt
Mr M.T. Moerane
Mr R.K. Muir (secretary)
Mr R.S. Naidoo
Mr N.E. Nuttall
Mr R. Tunmer (chairman)

Consultants

Prof W.M. Kgware
Prof L.W. Lanham
Dr E.G. Malherbe
Dr W.G. McConkey
Mr C. Nettleton
Prof F.K. Peters
Mr G.W. Tabor

Spro-cas Legal Commission

Mr H.J. Bhengu
Mr J.F. Coaker
Prof C.J.R. Dugard (secretary)
Mr C. Kinghorn
Mr W. Lane
Mr N.M. MacArthur
Prof D.B. Molteno
Mr C. Plewman
Adv K. Schwietering
Mr Jack Unterhalter (chairman)
Prof B. van Niekerk
Mr E.M. Wentzel
Mr A. Williamson

Spro-cas Political Commission

Mr T.V.R. Beard
Mr Leo Boyd
Dr the Hon E.H. Brookes
Mrs N.J.C. Charton
Dr T.R.H. Davenport
Dr Z.F. de Beer
Mr R.M. de Villiers
Dr W.B. de Villiers
Mr A.B. du Toit
Prof A.M. Hugo
Mr G. Lawrie
Mr Leo Marquard
Prof A.S. Mathews (chairman)
Mr J. Moloto
Prof D.B. Molteno
Rev C.F. Beyers Naudé
Dr W.F. Nkomo
Mr Alan Paton
Dr R. Turner
Mr P. van der Merwe
Dr D. Welsh (secretary)
Dr O.D. Wollheim
Mr D.J. Woods
Dr Denis Worrall

Consultants

Mr J. du P. Basson M.P.
Dr G.F. Jacobs M.P.

Spro-cas Social Commission

Note: This Commission was reconstituted after the first year

Dr A. Boraine
Mr André Brink
Chief Gatsha Buthelezi
Mr W.A. de Klerk
Mr P. Devitt
Mr L. Douwes Dekker
Mr Colin Gardner
Prof W.D. Hammon-Tooke
Mr B.A. Khoapa
Prof H. Lever
Mrs Fatima Meer
Prof C.L.S. Nyembezi
Prof N.J.J. Olivier
Rev J. Polley
Rev D. Poynton
Prof J.V.O. Reid (chairman)
Mr E.A. Saloojee
Mr L. Schlemmer (secretary)
Dr F. van Zyl Slabbert
Prof H.W. van der Merwe
Prof H.L. Watts
Dr M.G. Whisson

Consultants

Miss Anne Hope
Mr M. Savage
Rev L. Rakale
Mrs H. Sibisi
Prof Monica Wilson

3 Working Papers, Reports and Background Papers

NOTE: Some of these have been published in the four Spro-cas Occasional Publications.

All Commissions (Ref: Gen)

1. The Purpose and strategy of Spro-cas.
2. Notes for the guidance of the commissions.
3. Membership of the commissions (first and revised)
4. Recommended background reading
5. Press reaction to Spro-cas (first and second)
6. Suggested terms of reference—all commissions.
7. Reports of the first meetings of the commissions.
8. Programme of meetings (first and second)
9. Reference material available from Spro-cas.
10. *Enkele Gedagtes oor Spro-cas:* W.A. van der Sandt.
11. Background Paper: *Industrial Society:* Dr E.F. Schumacher.
12. Progress Report on Spro-cas to 30 September 1969.
13. Report on meeting of the Economics Commission: 26-28 September 1969.
14. Distribution of Documents 1.
15. Distribution of Documents 2.
16. Distribution of Documents 3.
17. *Address by Chief M.G. Buthelezi:* 11 June 1970.
18. Distribution of Documents 4.
19. *Black Souls in White Skins:* reprint from SASO Newsletter.
20. Spro-cas Publications Programme: Preliminary Notice.
21. Distribution of Documents: 5.
22. Progress Report to 4/4/71.
23. Spro-cas 2. Memorandum
24. Reactions to Education Report (1/12/71).
25. Reactions to Social Report (20/6/72).
26. Reactions to Church Report (20/11/72).

Church Commission (Ref. Ch)

1. Minutes of meeting: 11 June 1969.
2. Introductory Paper: *The Lordship of Christ:* Dr C.W. Cook.

3. Notice of meeting: 16-17 August 1969.
4. Background paper: *Church and World:* Professor B. Johanson.
5. Background paper: *Statistics of South African Churches:* Dr. E. Strassberger.
6. Background paper: *Denominationalism:* Rev. J.W. de Gruchy.
7. Background paper: *Hidden Presuppositions:* Rev. J.D. Davies.
8. Notes on discussions: 16-17 August 1969.
9. Minutes of meeting: 16-17 August 1969.
10. Practical suggestions for implementing the Message's principles.
11. Names and addresses of members of the commission.
12. Background paper: Suggestions for the Church Commission: *Mainly Attempts in Theological Diagnosis:* Rev. J.D. Davies.
13. Notice of meeting: 27-28 November 1969.
14. Report of the Western Cape working group, November 1969.
15. Report of the Transvaal working group, November 1969.
16. Report of the Border working group, November 1969.
17. Suggested outline for the report of the Church Commission.
18. Minutes of the meeting: 27-28 November 1969.
19. Draft report to the Strategy Commission: *Change in the Church.*
20. Draft report to the Strategy Commission: *Black Bargaining Power.*
21. Draft paper: *Structures:* Dr J.W. de Gruchy.
22. Notice of meeting: 16-17 April 1970.
23. Draft Introduction: Rev. D. Tutu.
24. Working paper: *Attitudes and Motives:* Rev. J.D. Davies.
25. *Discrimination:* working paper by Cape Town working group.
26. Working paper: *Clericalisation:* R. Ellis.
27. Working paper: *Mission of the Church:* Border Working group.
28. Draft paper: *State and Church:* Dr E. Strassberger.
29. Minutes of the meeting: 16-17 April 1970.
30. Notice of meeting: 28-29 July 1970.
31. Draft paper: *Mission of the Church:* Dr D.W. Bandey.
32. *Draft Report of the Commission:* First Portion.
33. *Suggestions for Immediate Concern.*
34. *Effects of Apartheid on the Church:* Mrs. S. Turner.
35. Minutes of the Meeting: 28-29 July 1970.
36. *Church and State:* Dr E. Strassberger and Rev D. Bax.
37. Report of the Commission: First Draft.
38. Report of the Commission: Second Draft.

Economics Commission (Ref Ec)

1. Notice of meeting: 26-28 September 1969.
2. Note on the concept of the Responsible Society.
3. Background Paper: *The Economics of Separate Development:* R.M. Siedle.
4. Background Paper: *The Trade Union Movement in S.A.:* L. Douwes-Dekker.
5. Background Paper: *Economics of the non-White minorities:* Dr A. Müller.
6. Papal Encyclical: *Mater et Magistra:* 1961.
7. Background Paper: *Some thoughts on the Economics Commission:* Dr G. M. Leistner.
8. Report of the meeting: 26-28 September 1969.
9. Background Paper: *African Trade Unions:* Dr F. Wilson.
10. Notice of meeting: 6-8 March 1970.
11. Working paper: *Capital and Enterprise:* Dr. A. L. Müller (revised).
12. *Labour Organisation:* Report of the sub-committee.
13. Working paper: *The Economics of Migrant Labour:* Dr F. Wilson.
14. Working paper: *The Colour Bar:* Professor S.T. van der Horst (revised).
15. Draft Outline: *The Role of Land:* D.C. Grice.
16. Working paper: *Data on Distribution of Income:* S. Archer.
17. *The Community of the Careless:* Dr A. Barker.
18. Report of the meeting: 6-8 March 1970.
19. Notice of meeting: 11-13 September 1970.
20. *Industrial Decentralisation in South Africa:* Dr Trevor Bell.
21. *Ethical and Philosophical Framework:* Sub-committee.
22. Background Paper: Report on 1970 SABRA Congress on Homeland Development: L. Schlemmer.
23. Report of the Meeting: 11-13 September 1970.
24. *Some Problems of Rural Development in Lesotho:* P. Devitt.
25. *Land:* Prof. R. Davies.
26. Background Paper: *African Resettlement:* Rev. C. Desmond.
27. Background Paper: *Decentralisation and Homeland Development:* W.H. Thomas
28. First draft report: November 1971.
29. Revised draft report: March 1972.

Education Commission (Ref Ed)

1. Notice of meeting: 22-24 August 1969.
2. Introductory paper: *Educational Implications of the Message:* Dr A.P. Hunter.

3.   Background paper: *Extracts from the Debate on the National Education Policy Bill.*
4.   *Blackout:* commentary on CNE: The Education League.
5.   *Some Aspects of Education in S.A.* (Occasional Publication No. 4 African Studies Programme, Wits, 1968).
6.   Background Paper: Summary of Castle: *Ancient Education and Today:* on Christian Education: Mr R. Tunmer.
7.   List of names and addresses of members of the commission.
8.   Report of the meeting: 22-24 August 1969.
9.   Working paper: *Education in South Africa:* Rev. C.B. Collins.
10. Background paper: *The Use of Films in Changing Attitudes:* Miss A. Adams.
11. Notice of meeting: 30 January—1 February 1970.
12. Working paper: *Immediate Education Steps:* Dr W.G. McConkey.
13. Working paper: *Mother Tongue Instruction in African Education:* Professor W.H. Lanham.
14. Christian National Education: Report of the sub-committee.
15. *Christelike-Nasionale Onderwys getoets aan Christelike Beginsels:* Dr. B. Engelbrecht.
16. Working paper: *Immediate Educational Steps:* Dr W.G. McConkey (revised).
17. Report of meeting: 30 January—1 February 1970.
18. Notice of meeting: 5-7 June 1970.
19. Draft Report of the Commission.
20. *Church and Private Schools:* Interim Report.
21. Report of meeting: 5-6 June 1970.
22. Report of the Commission: Second Draft.
23. Report of the Commission: Third Draft.

Legal Commission (Ref: L)

1.   Preliminary notice: 30:6:69.
2.   Working paper: *Effects of Apartheid on the Whites:* J. Coaker.
3.   Working paper: *Effects of Apartheid on the Courts:* N.M. MacArthur.
4.   Working paper: *Effects of Apartheid:* Anon.
5.   Working paper: *The Police Force in South African Society:* Dr B. van Niekerk.
6.   Background paper: *Capital Punishment:* P.R. Randall.
7.   Notice of meeting: 22-24 May 1970.
8.   Working paper: *Change and Methods of Change:* E.M. Wentzel.
9.   Working paper: *Effect of Apartheid on Administrative Bodies:* C. Kinghorn.

10. Working paper: *Effects of Apartheid on non-whites:* W. Lane and A. Williamson.
11. Working paper: *Effects of Apartheid on our inherited understanding of the Law:* J. Unterhalter.
12. Working paper: *Change and methods of Change:* Professor D.B. Molteno.
13. Report of meeting: 22-23 May 1970.
14. Background paper: *The Liberal Heritage of the Law:* Professor C. Dugard.
15. Draft Introduction to Report.

Political Commission (Ref: Pol)

1. Notice of meeting: 29-31 August 1969.
2. Introductory paper: *Notes on the Political Commission:* G. Lawrie.
3. Note on the concept of the Responsible Society.
4. *The Future of Southern Africa:* Lusaka statement (photocopy).
5. Leading articles: *Star* 14:7:69, *Vaderland* 15:7:69, *Rand Daily Mail* 23:7:69 (photocopies).
6. Supplementary list of suggested readings.
7. Memorandum on the franchise submitted by E. Goldstein.
8. Names and addresses of members of the commission.
9. Report of meeting: 29-31 August 1969.
10. Report of the sub-committee: *The Present Political Situation and the Problem of sharing political power.*
11. Working paper: *Breaches of Ethical Concepts:* Messrs. Marquard, Nkomo and Wollheim.
12. *The Arguments in favour of the Common Roll:* Dr Edgar Brookes.
13. Notice of meeting: 20-22 February 1970.
14. Working paper: *The Rule of Law:* Professor A.S. Mathews.
15. Minutes of sub-committee meeting: 28-30 November 1969.
16. Working paper: *The Primary Ethical Concepts Relating to Political Life:* Dr Edgar Brookes.
17. Working paper: *The political Role of the Churches in South Africa:* Dr W.B. de Villiers.
18. Background Paper: *Die Federale Gedagte:* J. du P. Basson M.P.
19. Working paper: *The Political Alternatives:* G. Lawrie.
20. Working paper: *Primary Ethical Concepts:* A.B. du Toit.
21. Working paper: *The Politics of Diversity:* Dr D. Worrall.
22. Report of the meeting: 20-22 February 1970.
23. *Political Systems in Multi-racial Societies:* K.A. Heard (SAIRR 1961).
24. Notice of meeting: 31 July-2 August 1970.

25. *Breaches of Ethical Concepts* (revision of Pol 11).
26. *Federalism:* G. Lawrie.
27. Working paper: *Student Reaction to the General Election and Student expectations about political development:* P. van der Merwe.
28. *The Enforcement of Civil Rights:* G. Lawrie.
29. *The Rule of Law:* Professor A.S. Mathews (revision of Pol 14).
30. *The Common Society:* Dr Edgar Brookes.
31. *Effective Participation in government:* A.B. du Toit.
32. *Political Role of the Churches* (revision of Pol 17).
33. *The Plural-State System as a direction of Change:* Dr D. Worrall.
34. *The Problem of Premises:* Professor M.H.H. Louw.
35. *Some Thoughts on the Common Society:* Mr. Alan Paton.
36. *The Relevance of Contemporary Radical Thought:* Dr R. Turner.
37. Report of the meeting: 31 July-2 August 1970.
38. *Breaches of Ethical Concepts* (revision of Pol. 25).
39. Working paper: *Political Vulnerabilities:* Dr W.B. de Villiers.
40. Notice of meeting: 12-14 February 1971.
41. *The Common Society Approach:* Prof. A.S. Mathews and Mr. Alan Paton.
42. *Effective Participation in Government* (continuation of Pol 31).
43. *The U.P. Plan for a New Realism:* Dr G.F. Jacobs M.P.
44. *The Significance of Local Government in a Plural Society:* Mrs. Nancy Charton.
45. *The S.A. Political Situation: Problems and Prospects:* Prof. W.B. Vosloo.
46. *Prospects of a U.P. Victory:* Prof. H. Lever.
47. *Political Role of the Churches* (revision of Pol 32).
48. *A Federal Response to Diversity:* Japie Basson M.P.
49. *Participatory Democracy and Worker's Control:* Dr R. Turner.
50. Minutes of the Meeting: 12-14 February, 1971.
51. Draft Report: June 1972
52. Statement by the Chairman of Commission: June 1973.

Social Commission (Ref: Soc).

1. Notice of meeting: 15-17 August 1969.
2. Introductory paper: *Notes on the Social Commission:* L. Schlemmer.
3. Names and addresses of members of the commission.
4. Report of meeting: 15-17 August 1969.
5. Background paper: *Use of Films in changing attitudes:* Miss A. Adams.
6. Working paper: *Poverty:* Professor H.L. Watts.
7. Working paper: *A Code of Personal Behaviour for Christians in Apartheid Society:* Rev. L. Rakale.

8. Working paper: *English-speaking White South Africans:* Mr C. Gardner.
9. Working paper: *Malnutrition:* Professor J.V.O. Reid.
10. Working paper: *Coloured Politics:* Dr M.G. Whisson.
11. Working paper: *Opportunities for Coloured People:* Dr M.G. Whisson.
12. Working paper: *Towards a reducation of inter-group tension and hostility:* Dr M.G. Whisson.
13. Working paper: *Education: Support for existing projects:* Mrs. R. Selsick.
14. Notice of meeting: 13-15 February 1970.
15. Working paper: *The New Community:* Rev. J. Polley.
16. Working paper: *Indian Society:* E.A. Saloojee.
17. Working paper: *The Bases of Apartheid:* L. Schlemmer.
18. Working paper: *Future Political Implications of Present Trends in S.A.* L. Schlemmer.
19. Working Paper: *The Social Consequences of Economic Development:* F. van Zyl Slabbert.
20. Working paper: *The Afrikaner: Contemporary Attitudes:* W.A. de Klerk.
21. Working paper: *Current Trends and policies relating to the Indian people:* Fatima Meer.
22. *African Attitudes:* notes on some interviews.
23. Working paper: *Some aspects of Culture and apartheid:* A. Brink.
24. *Model, Experimental Church:* Draft paper for the SACC Strategy Comm: T. Kotze.
25. *Sport;* Draft paper for the Strategy Commission.
26. Resource paper: *African Attitudes:* Anon.
27. Report of the second meeting: 13-15 February 1970.
28. *Handbook on Multi-Racial Congregations:* Rev. R. Robertson.
29. Notice of meeting: 12-14 June 1970.
30. Working paper: *The Race Factor in separate development:* Professor N. Rhoodie.
31. Working paper: *A Sociological view of separate ethno-national development:* Professor N. Rhoodie.
32. *Poverty:* H.L. Watts (Revision of Soc 6).
33. *Coloured People of the Cape: Current attitudes:* Dr M. Whisson (Revision of Soc 10).
34. *Role of the white student community:* Clive Smith.
35. Background paper: *The Role of Social Scientists in South Africa: Problems of Involvement in a Plural Society:* Professor H.W. van der Merwe.
36. *The Future of the Commission:* Letter from the Director.
37. *Malnutrition:* Professor J.V.O. Reid (Revision of Soc 9).

38. The Future of the Commission 2: Letter from the director.
39. *A Practical Programme to reduce Inter-group tensions:* Prof. H. Lever.
40. *General Remarks on Nationalism as a factor in Race Relations in South Africa:* Prof. N.J. Rhoodie.
41. Report on Steering Committee Meeting: 13 January 1971.
42. Notice of Meeting: 30 April—2 May 1971.
43. *Cultural Diversity and Politics in S.A.:* Dr F. van Zyl Slabbert.
44. *Education and Social Change:* M.J. Ashley.
45. *Social Organisations available for Change:* Dr M.G. Whisson.
46. *Strategies for Change:* L. Schlemmer.
47. *Programme for Change:* L. Douwes Dekker.
48. Draft introduction to final report.

Co-ordinating Committee (Ref: Co)

1. Minutes of meeting: 14 June 1969.
2. Minutes of meeting: 6 September 1969.
3. *A Tentative Framework for Co-ordination:* Memo from the Director.

4. List of Publications

The following publications have been issued by Spro-cas 1, Spro-cas 2, the Black Community Programmes and Ravan Press. The figures in brackets show the approximate number of copies distributed at 1 September, 1973.

SPRO-CAS 1

1.	Anatomy of Apartheid (ed. Peter Randall) Dec. 1970	(5 295)
2.	South Africa's Minorities (ed. Peter Randall) Feb. 1971	(4 220)
3.	Directions of Change in South African Politics (ed. Peter Randall) March 1971	(4 470)
4.	Some Implications of Inequality (ed. Peter Randall) April 1971	(4 320)
5.	Education beyond Apartheid (ed. Peter Randall) Aug. 1971	(5 140)
5(a)	Opvoeding Verby Apartheid (red. Peter Randall) Aug. 1971	(520)
6.	Towards Social Change (ed. Peter Randall) Dec. 1971 (reprinted Jan. 1973)	(4 600)
6(a)	Maatskaplike Vooruitgang (red. Peter Randall) Feb. 1972	(300)
7.	Power, Privilege and Poverty (ed. Peter Randall) June 1972 (reprinted June 1973)	(4 510)
8.	Apartheid and the Church (ed. Peter Randall) Aug. 1972	(4 170)
9.	Law, Justice and Society (ed. Peter Randall) Nov. 1972	(2 700)
10.	South Africa's Political Alternatives (ed. Peter Randall) June 1973	(2 950)

SPRO-CAS 2

1.	The Eye of the Needle — R. Turner, May 1972 (banned March 1973)	(3 470)
2.	Cry Rage — James Matthews and Gladys Thomas, Dec, 1972 (banned March 1973)	(4 140)
3.	Migrant Labour in South Africa — F. Wilson (published jointly by S.A. Council of Churches and Spro-cas), Jan 1973	(3 150)
4.	White Liberation — ed. Horst Kleinschmidt — Feb. 1973	(1 300)
5.	Fear or Freedom — April 1973	(3 000)
6.	Sing for our Execution — Wopko Jensma, June 1973	(1 320)
7.	Outlook on a Century, eds. F. Wilson and D. Perrot (published jointly by Spro-cas and Lovedale Press), July 1973	(n/a)
8.	Contact Series: a series of communications designed to assist change agencies.	(n/a)

BLACK COMMUNITY PROGRAMMES

1.   Black Viewpoint — ed. Steve Biko, Sept. 1972   (4 250)
2.   Black Review 1972 — ed. Bennie Khoapa, March 1973   (±3 300)
3.   Handbook of Black Organisations, July 1973   (600)

Note: The report of the Spro-cas Economics Commission has been
published in German: *Südafrika: Macht, Armut und Privilegien,* Texte 7 of
Dienste in Übersee (July 1973).
   A Dutch edition of *Cry Rage,* with translations by Prof Rothuizen, has been
published by J.V. Kok.
   A French edition of *Cry Rage,* is planned by a French publisher.
   Various translations of Spro-cas reports into Dutch are planned.

   The total distribution figures of Spro-cas Publications have grown as
follows:

5/7/71	8 920
17/1/71	17 291
3/7/72	26 767
20/9/72	32 621
4/12/72	38 745
10/5/73	57 445
1/7/73	65 000
1/9/73	70 000

Other   Published   Material   of   Spro-cas   2

Background Papers

1.   Violence in Southern Africa: the House of Lords Debate (summary by
     Bishop John Carter).
2.   Student Protest: The Conflicting Polarities (prepared by Peter Randall)
3.   Migrant Labour: The Canker in our Society (prepared by John Kane-
     Berman).
4.   The Spro-cas Education Report: one Year Later (prepared by F.E.
     Auerbach).
5.   Rule by Law or Rule by Police? (prepared by John Kane-Berman).

6. Conscientious Objection (prepared by Dot Cleminshaw).
7. Citizen Participation (prepared by Maeder Osler and Ivor Shapiro).
8. A Cultural Effort for Change: Andre Brink.
   (Total Distribution $\pm$ 30 000)

Discussion Papers

1. Universities and Social Change — Geoff Budlender.
2. Dimbaza Rations: a comparison with Boer War Concentration Camps — Dot Cleminshaw.

Study Aids

1. Education beyond Apartheid (prepared by Peter Randall).
2. Towards Social Change (prepared by Elim Study group).
3. Power, Privilege and Poverty (prepared by Peter Randall).
4. Apartheid and the Church (prepared by John de Gruchy).
5. Law, Justice and Society (prepared by Ivor Shapiro).
   (Total distribution $\pm$20 000)

Dossiers (press articles, photographs etc)
(prepared by Horst Kleinschmidt)

1. South-West Africa (Namibia)
2. The Crisis in Labour Relations
3. Student-Police Confrontation (for NUSAS)
4. Strike!
5. One Week in May
6. 'Society of Violence and Fear'
7. Black Students Dissent
8. Schlebusch 1 and 2

Total distribution figures of Publications and other published material:

Publications	70 000
Background Papers	30 000
Study Aids	20 000
Dossiers	5 000
Total	125 000

Other resource material produced includes poster, calendars, study kits, reports on seminars, reprints of lectures and articles, simulation games, and casette recordings of the lectures given in the Need for Reform series (February - June 1973):

1. The Need for Rural Reform — Dr Anthony Barker
2. The Need for Reform in the Church — Archbishop Denis Hurley
3. The Need for Social and Educational Reform — Andre Brink
4. The Need for Legal Reform — a panel of legal experts
5. The Need for Labour Reform — Mr Barney Dladla, Mr David Hemson, Mr Loet Douwes Dekker
6. The Need for Social and Political Reform — Dr Beyers Naudè.
7. Change in the Church — Dr Manas Butelezi
8. Maatskaplike Verandering — Dr F. van Zyl Slabbart

(The lecture on Economic Reform by Dr F. Wilson was unfortunately not recorded.)
Also available is a cassette recording of the inaugural Helen Suzman Lecture on Equality in Education, given by Peter Randall at the Johannesburg College of Education, June '73.

Some Planned Future Publications

1. Nadine Gordimer: *The Black Interpreters - an Introduction to African Writing* (Spro-cas/Ravan 1973)
2. N. Chabani Manganyi: *Being-Black-in-the-World* (Spro-cas/Ravan, 1973)
3. D.C.S. Oosthuizen: *The Ethics of Illegal Action* (Spro-cas/Ravan, 1973)
4. Douglas Bax: *Church and State in South Africa* (Ravan, 1974)
5. W.H. Thomas (ed.): *Labour Relations* (Ravan, 1973)
6. Peter Walshe: *African Nationalsim in South Africa*

Ravan Publications

1. Wopko Jensma: Sing for our Execution (published jointly with Ophir) (June 1973)
2. Ophir 17 (published jointly with Ophir) (June 1973)
3. Management Responsibility and African Employment (published on behalf of investigating panel) (June 1973).

5 Financing of Spro-cas

1969	Spro-cas 1	R13 810
1970	Spro-cas 1	R12 258
1971	Spro-cas 1	R17 071
1972	Spro-cas 1	R 1 094
1972	Spro-cas 2	R45 606
	BCP	R17 920
1973 (budget)	Spro-cas 2	R45 000
	BCP	R50 300
	Total 1969 - 1973	R203 059

The major donors of the 3 Spro-cas projects were:

Kirchlicher Entwicklungsdienst	R39 062
Landskirche Hessen-Nassau	R30 969
Kom over de Brug	R24 340
Church of Norway	R23 781
Group Chairman's Fund	R22 000
Christian Aid	R20 099
Maurice Webb Trust	R14 000
Christian Fellowship Trust	R 9 166
Church of Sweden Mission	R 7 500
H.E.K.S.	R 4 323
Rissik Trust	R 4 000
Vrije Universiteit, Amsterdam	R 1 400

Total donations received from South African Churches amounted to approximately: R1 200 00

6   Selected Documents

The history of Spro-cas, and the development of thinking within the project, can be traced through the following selected documents:

1. The Purpose and Strategy of this project (Gen. 1, March 1969)
2. Progress Report to 30 Sept. 1969 (Gen. 12, October 1969)
3. Progress Report to 2 April 1971 (Gen. 22, April 1971)
4. Some Reactions to the Spro-cas Education Report (Gen. 24, 1 Dec. 1971)
5. Some Reactions to the Spro-cas Social Report (Gen. 25, 20 June 1972)
6. Some Reactions to the Spro-cas Church Report (Gen. 26, 16 Nov. 1972)
7. Tentative Proposals for Spro-cas 2 (Special Programme for Christian Action in Society) (Sept. 9, 1971)
8. Black Community Programmes: Tentative Suggestions for Action (30 Sept. 1971)
9. Special Programme for Christian Action in Society (Spro-cas2) (Dec. 1971)
10. Spro-cas: Five Biblical Principles (Sept. 1972)
11. Spro-cas BCP: Report and Budget Proposals (Sept. 1972)
12. Spro-cas white programmes: Some working notes (Oct. 1972)
13. Economic Change in South Africa; Spro-cas release (Nov. 1972)
14. Spro-cas: Motivations and Assumptions (March 1973)
15. A Programme for Social Change: preliminary draft (May 1973)
16. Spro-cas Political Report: release (June 1973)
17. Open Letter to the Leader of the Opposition (August 1973)

Note: See appendix where these documents are reprinted.

7. Spro-cas Staff

Spro-cas 1
Director: Peter Randall (Mar. 1969 - Dec. 1973)
Secretary: Alethea Maclagan (Mar. 1969 - Feb. 1971)
               Patricia Kirkman (Mar. 1971 - Dec. 1973)

Spro-cas 2
Director: Peter Randall (Jan. 1972 - Dec. 1973)
Communications
Director: Danie van Zyl (Jan. 1972 - Dec. 1973)
Secretaries: Patricia Kirkman (Jan. 1972 - Dec. 1973)
               Ilona Kleinschmidt (April 1972 - Dec. 1973)
Organisers: Neville Curtis (Mar. 1972 - Dec. 1972)
               Horst Kleinschmidt (April 1972 - Dec. 1973)
               Ivor Shapiro (April 1972 - Dec. 1973)
               Nikki Westcott (Nov. 1972 - Dec. 1973)
Messenger: Lazarus Modiakgotlo (Aug. 1972 - Dec. 1973)
Temporary/   Patricia Goodwin   Isobel Randall
part time: Jimmy Cochrane   Helmine van Zyl
               June Pym   Marie-Jeanne Wytenburg
               Des Adendorff   Frances Hoffeldt
               Bruce Sandilands (accountant)
Type-setter: Beulah Cassim (Jan. 1972 - Dec. 1972, thereafter Ravan)

BCP.   (January 1972 - March 1973: thereafter autonomous body)
Director: Bennie A. Khoapa
Secretary: Hester Fortune
Field Workers: Steve B. Biko and Bokwe Mafuna
Assistant: Samantha Moodley

Ravan Press

The press was established at the beginning of 1973 as an outgrowth of the Christian Institute's printing unit which developed primarily to meet Sprocas's production meeds.

Staff
Director: Danie van Zyl
Printers: Billy Lazarus
               Ben Welkom

Type-setters:	Beulah Cassim
	Brenda Trimmel
	Pam Cardin
Binders:	Boya Jack
	Gabriel Phale
General	Mrs J. Dickinson
assistants:	Lorraine Masana
Collators	Veronica Romain
	Ann Swartz
	Josephine Khaile
Part time	Mrs I.M. Randall
assistants:	Miss Violet Walker

8   Future Plans

A reading of the selected documents contained in section 6 above indicates three clear directions for future work which arise organically from the Spro-cas experience. In the first place there is the emergence of an autonomous black organisation from the Spro-cas Black Community Programmes. It is hoped that this will become a permanent body, pursuing the same kind of objectives as the BCP itself. (see Document 11).

Secondly, the kind of publishing and the variety of communications produced by Spro-cas has been valuable in terms both of understanding our situation and of working for change. Ravan Press was established to meet the production needs of such material and it is intended that the press should continue as an independent publishing and communications company after Spro-cas itself ends.

Thirdly, there is a need for some of the functions which Spro-cas has partly helped to fulfil in the white community to be continued in a systematic way.

These functions include contact and co-ordination between those working for change, the clarifying of goals and strategies for change, the pooling of resources and skills, and the promoting of radical alternatives to the present social order. To provide a framework for the achievement of such tasks, Spro-cas has proposed the establishment of a Programme for Social Change (see document 15).

9   Acknowledgements

It is impossible to list individually those hundreds of people who have
assisted in the work of Spro-cas. They include the members and consultants
of the study commissions, particularly those who drafted the reports; those
who helped the commissions by supplying information and memoranda; the
director, staff and members of the Christian Institute; the South African
Council of Churches; printers, artists, photographers and cartoonists; those
who served on the various Spro-cas 2 action groups and panels; those who
suggested research and action projects and those who participated in them;
many individual church leaders and laypeople; church groups like the Catholic Justice and Peace Commissions, the Anglican Human Relations Programme, the Methodist Youth Department, the Swiss Mission, and others;
bodies whose co-operation and support have meant so much to Spro-cas, like
the Black Sash, NUSAS, the Wages Commissions, various SRC's; those who
have spoken and lectured from Spro-cas platforms; the journalists and commentators who have helped to disseminate the thinking generated by Spro-
cas; those bookshops which have stocked and sold Spro-cas publications; and
those many others who have helped in an astonishing variety of ways, from
preparing background papers and participating in informal discussions on
strategy to selling books at conferences and providing transport and accommodation.

Above all, we are grateful for the friendship and co-operation of the director
and staff of the Black Community Programmes, for the faith and generosity
of those who provided the funds to make both Spro-cas and the BCP possible,
and for the sponsorship of the S.A. Council of Churches and the Christian
Institute, who thereby demonstrated their commitment to work for social renewal in South Africa.

APPENDIX

DOCUMENT 1

THE PURPOSE AND STRATEGY OF THIS PROJECT

A. The Purpose

1. The Message to the People of South Africa is our point of departure. A significant body of Christians in our country has stated that our present social order (apartheid) is an ideology that is opposed to Christianity, and that Christianity demands love and association between people and groups rather than hostility and segregation.

What are the implications of these viewpoints? Is it possible to create a social order in South Africa based on the integrative thrusts of love and association? Would the attempt result in such disruption and enmity that we would have a situation worse than it is now? If the attempt has to be made, how do we suggest realistic ways of bringing about integration in our educational system, our political structures, our economic system?

Is some form of political and social integration inevitable, anyway, and should we be looking for policies and programmes which will bring about the transition to a common society enjoying the loyalty of all our people in ways that are as harmonious and orderly as possible? These questions which are implied by the Message provide the raison d'etre for the project.

Another way of putting it is to say that we are seeking to make a positive contribution to the creation of a better social order in South Africa, one based on Christian values such as justice and opportunity for all. We wish to contribute to and participate in dialogue, and dialogue begins with the posing of basic questions.

B The Composition and Task of the Commissions

2. It would be presumptuous to suggest that only Christians can find the solutions to our problems. We believe that the Spirit of God also expresses itself through people who are not Christians. We do not believe that it is right to suggest that there could be specifically Christian political policies, educational programmes or economic systems. Christians themselves differ on these things. But we do believe that some policies, programmes and systems are closer than others to Christian ethics, and we believe also that it is right to say that these former are more likely to gain acceptance from those belonging to other faiths or to no faith who desire a South Africa based on such values as

justice and equal opportunity. It should be clear from this that we would not suggest the imposition of specifically 'Christian' policies, if there are any, on a multi-religious society such as ours.

For these reasons we have invited a number of non-Christians to serve on the commissions where we have felt that they are likely to accept the basic thrust of this project, and where we know that they have abilities and imsights which will assist us in our task. We have been gratified by the response from such people.

3.   The Message is a theological critique of apartheid; but with the exception of the theological commission, the commissions are not expected to concern themselves primarily with theology. Their first task will probably be to define a social-ethical basis for the working of society. The members are composed of experts in the areas of economics, education, law, politics and society, and they will, we anticipate, be engaged in a hard-headed and realistic assessment of the implications of the Message. Occasionally, of course, experts in these areas will also be theologians and we are fortunate in having secured the services of a number of people with this dual background.

4.   We have tried to include on the commissions as wide a range of viewpoints as possible. We are endeavouring to be open-minded and objective about the results of their study, and do not necessarily expect unanimity in the findings of each commission. We do not believe that there are simple and straightforward practical solutions to our problems.

Since we do not wish to initiate a debate ab initio on the principles behind the Message in each commission, we have not sought to persuade those who have appeared unable to accept these principles at all.

As the project proceeds we shall, however, attempt to establish and maintain dialogue with individuals and groups representative of viewpoints not included in the commissions.

5.   We feel that the time is ripe for this project. The public debate on the morality of apartheid is never far below the surface, and there are indications that it is now beginning to resume with vigour. A great many South Africans are perplexed and confused and would welcome new leads based firmly on morally justifiable principles. An example of this is the position of our people who are classified 'Coloured': When the Prime Minister admits that his government has no 'solution' to the 'Coloured problem', this is an invitation to people who are concerned about our country to do some earnest thinking aimed at finding, and suggesting, possible solutions.

C   Christian Social Principles

6. It may be useful at this stage to indicate in broad terms the ethical concern in relation to the social order which we believe is inherent in Christianity (and therefore the Message), which concern we share with many other non-Christians and is a common basis for collaboration.

The following quotation from Castle and the digest of Temple may serve as examples of the thinking of two Christians reflecting upon the existing order.

'When we consider the nature of a Christian man or a Christian society we think in terms of personality, integrity, discipline, and self-discipline, freedom and restraint, obligation and responsibility, thinking and working, knowledge and understanding, co-operation, neighbourliness, love. All these factors have to be thought out and worked out ... under the guiding principles that persons are intrinsically valuable, that persons should love one another, that persons must be socially responsible ......'   (Castle: *Ancient Education and To-day* p. 208)

The following digest of some of the main points in W.Temple's *Christianity and the Social Order* (Pelican) will further help to indicate something of our attitude:

(i)   The Church must announce Christian principles and point out where the existing social order is in conflict with them. It must then pass on the task of re-shaping the existing order.

(ii)   It is fundamental to the Christian position that men should have freedom even though they abuse it.

(iii)   The most fundamental requirement of any political and economic system is not that it shall express love, though that is desirable, nor that it shall express justice, though that is the first ethical demand to be made upon it, but that it shall supply some reasonable measure of security against murder, robbery and starvation. If it can be said with real probability that a proposed scheme would in fact, men being what they are, fail to provide that security, that scheme is doomed.

(iv)   There is no such thing as a Christian social ideal, to which we should conform our society as closely as possible ... No one really wants to live in the ideal state as depicted by someone else ... but (Christianity) supplies something of far more value — namely principles on which we can begin to act in every possible situation.

(v)   The primary principle ... must be respect for every person simply as a person. The first aim of social progress must be to give the fullest possible scope for the exercise of all powers and qualities which are distinctly personal; and of these the most fundamental is deliberate choice. Consequently society must be so arranged as to give to every citizen the maximum opportunity for making deliberate choices and the best possible training for the use of that opportunity. To train citizens in the capacity for freedom and to give them scope for free action is the supreme end of all true politics. But man ... can be trusted to abuse his freedom ... so there must be the restraint of law, as long as men have any selfishness left in them. Law exists to preserve and extend real freedom.

(vi)   The family is the initial form of man's social life and its preservation and security is the first principle of social welfare. The Christian conception of men as members in the family of God forbids the notion that freedom may be used for self-interest. It is justified only when it expresses itself through fellowship; and a free society must be so organised as to make this effectual; in other words it must be rich in sectional groupings or fellowship within the harmony of the whole ... This point has great political importance; for (personal) relationships exist in the whole network of communities, associations and fellowship. It is in these that the real wealth of human life consists. If then it is the function of the state to promote human well-being, it must foster these many groupings.

(vii)   The combination of freedom and fellowship as principles of social life issues in the obligation of service ... A man must chiefly serve his own immediate community ... but always checking this narrower service by the wider claims, so that in serving the smaller community he never injures the larger.

(viii)   Freedom, fellowship, service — these are the three principles of a Christian social order, derived from the still more fundamental Christian postulants that man is a child of God and is destined for a life of eternal fellowship with him.

We do not suggest that these views are definitive, but they are given here in the hope that they will help to stimulate thought and discussion. There are many works which might have the same effect. Some of them are suggested in the bibliography.

May 1969

DOCUMENT 2

SPRO-CAS: PROGRESS REPORT TO 30 SEPTEMBER 1969

1 Public Reaction

In July and August extensive coverage was given in the South African press to the aims and the nature of the project. Leading articles appeared in *The Star, The Rand Daily Mail, The Daily News, Hoofstad, Die Transvaler,* and *Die Vaderland,* amongst other papers. Political columnists in a number of newspapers commented on the project.

The reaction in the English-language press was generally fovourable, that in the Afrikaans press generally hostile, although a columnist writing in *Die Beeld* said, 'They sincerely wish the results to be scientific and objective and towards this end they have tried to get the widest possible representation in the country.'

The Prime Minister referred in disparaging tones to Spro-cas during the course of a major policy speech at Nylstroom early in August, and again when addressing the Natal Congress of the Nationalist Party on 22 September.

The project was referred to, either in reports or leading articles, in a number of publications, particularly church and ecumenical journals. These included the *Christian Recorder, Kairos* (the organ of the South African Council of Churches), the *South African Outlook,* and *Pro Veritate.* The latter carried an editorial on the project, as well as an article by the director of Spro-cas.

Two summaries of the press reaction to Spro-cas were distributed to the members of the commissions.

The director of Spro-cas was invited to speak to a number of church gatherings about the work of the commissions and the aims of the project.

Several members of the public reacted personally to the public announcement regarding the project. In this way two or three new members were gained for the commissions, while a number of written documents were received. Several of these, including *Enkele Gedagtes oor Spro-cas* by Mr W.A. van der Sandt of Johannesburg and *The Economics of Separate Development* by Mr R.M. Siedle of Netherlands Bank, were duplicated and distributed to the members of the commissions.

Many people called at the Spro-cas office to discuss the project and offer suggestions, some of which have been adopted.

2   Composition of the Commissions

There have been minor modifications in the membership of the commissions since the last progress report was issued in May. A corrected list was issued and sent to all members of the different commissions.

The Church Commission was reconstituted to differentiate it from the Theological Commission of the South African Council of Churches. This brought about a reduction in membership from 39 to 29, with three consultants. The former arrangement had proved unwieldy.

Some people who had previously agreed to serve on commissions reconsidered their positions and decided to withdraw. This usually appeared to be the result of pressure having been brought to bear on them by employers or other authorities.

The total number of people involved is now more than 140, comprising 112 members of the commissions and 30 consultants. They are drawn from nearly all the ethnic and cultural groups in South Africa, 17 different universities and university colleges, and about 16 different Christian denominations. A very wide range of occupations is represented. The Students' Representative Councils of nearby universities were invited to appoint observer/consultants to attend the meetings of the Education, Economics, Political and Social Commissions. The Universities of the Witwatersrand, Natal, Cape Town, Stellenbosch, The University College of the Western Cape and the Johannesburg College of Education all accepted the invitation and the participation of their student delegates in the discussions was a valuable feature of the meetings.

3.   Background Material

Forty-eight documents have been distributed to the members of the commissions. These include papers of a general nature sent to all the commissions (for example: a list of suggested background reading, summaries of press reaction to Spro-cas, a list of reference material available from the Spro-cas office etc.), and 14 background papers or memoranda prepared by individual members of the commissions. These range from *Statistics of South African Churches* (Dr E. Strassberger) and *The Trade Union Movement in South Africa* (Mr L. Douwes Dekker) to *Educational Implications of the Message* (Dr A.P. Hunter) and *Notes on the Political Commission* (Mr G. Lawrie). Permission was granted by Dr E.F. Schumacher, British Director of Statistics, for his paper on *Industrial Society* to be duplicated and distributed to all participants in the project. Dr Schumacher discusses many of the basic issues which the commissions are considering.

Several books and other printed publications were also distributed when it was felt they were useful for the members of particular commissions and when it was possible to obtain them free or at a reduced price. There is no provision in the budget for this type of expenditure so that it has not been possible to obtain and distribute as much material as we would wish.

A small collection of reference and background material is being built up in the Spro-cas office. Funds again are inadequate for a reasonably complete collection to be undertaken. Since 1 April press clippings have been kept, and these are classified according to the different commissions, whose members may consult or borrow them.

A complete list of all documents and books distributed by 12 September was sent to members of the different commissions.

4   Co-ordination

The reports of the meetings of the different commissions have been circulated amongst all the members and consultants. The director of the project has attended the meetings and where necessary has sought to prevent unprofitable duplication and to suggest where co-operation between different commissions would be desirable.

The steering committee consisting of the Rt. Rev. B.B. Burnett, the Rev. C.F.B. Naudè, Mr J.S. Paton and Mr P. Randall, has continued to meet when necessary to review progress and take decisions regarding future plans.

A co-ordination committee of sixteen members drawn from the different commissions met in June to consider plans for the first round of meetings of the commissions and again in September to review progress and give preliminary thought to the questions of communication and implementation as well as to problems of co-ordination generally.

5   Meetings of the Commissions

(Note: The relevant reports have been circulated to members and consultants of the commissions, but have not been more widely distributed since at this stage they are regarded as confidential.)

Attendances at the first meetings of the full commissions during August and September were very pleasing. Twenty were present at the meeting of the Church Commission, held in Johannesburg on 16-17 August; sixteen at the Economics Commission, Johannesburg 26-28 September; eighteen at the Education Commission, Johannesburg, 22-24 August; nineteen at the Political Commission, Cape Town, 29-31 August; eighteen at the Social Commission, Botha's Hill, 15-17 August.

Two principal tasks were envisaged for these first meetings, and in each case these were accomplished. The first task, through general discussion and a consideration of the documents which had been previously circulated was to reach clarity and agreement on the aims and function of the commission (i.e. adoption of terms of reference). The second was to survey the area to be covered, to select the most important aspects for further study, and to allocate tasks, involving the preparation of relevant material.

Each commission adopted terms of reference, based on the suggestions previously sent out, and went some way towards demarcating its area of study. More than fifty tasks were allocated, either to sub-groups or to individual members of commissions. These are, generally, the production of draft papers or working memoranda which will be circulated before the commissions meet again which will be during February - March 1970, in the case of the Education, Social and Political commissions. The topics range from Christian-National Education and the Rule of Law to a study of the Political Role of the Churches and an analysis of the Social Forces underlying Apartheid.

A number of working group meetings will be held during the next few months in order to prepare documents for the next round of meetings. The first meetings were similarly preceeded by meetings of working groups.

The Church Commission divided into three groups, located in the Transvaal, the Border area and the Western Cape, to prepare reports for the next full meeting of the commission which will be held in Johannesburg on 27-28 November 1969.

The Johannesburg members of the Legal Commission met during July and, having adopted terms of reference, divided the tasks among the members of the commission, who are at present engaged in drafting memoranda and papers. When these have been circulated a meeting of the full commission will be called, probably in November 1969.

The Economics, Education, Political and Social commissions met from a Friday evening to the following Sunday noon. Two of the meetings were residental, which resulted in approximately twenty hours being available for work.

In order to encourage full and frank discussion the meetings were as informal as possible, and in the case of the Social Commission almost entirely unstructured.

Professor J.V.O. Reid was elected chairman of the Social Commission, Professor A.M. Hugo of the Political Commission, Professor I.D. MacCrone of the Education Commission and Mr Jack Unterhalter of the Legal Commission. Mr I.S. Haggie agreed to take the chair for the first meeting of the Economics Commission. The following agreed to act as secretaries to the different commissions: the Rev. J.W. de Gruchy — Church. Dr Francis Wilson — Economics; Mr R.K. Muir — Education; Rev. John Henderson — Legal; Mr David Welsh — Political; Mr Lawrie Schlemmer — Social.

The members of the commissions showed themselves to be anxious to avoid mere repetition of work done by other groups and organisations and to be as realistic as possible in their approach. The question of the eventual communication of the results of their work also featured largely in their deliberations.

It was generally agreed that effective means of achieving change was an important issue for each commission to explore. The S.A. Council of Churches is to establish a commission on strategy for change, and it is expected that this commission will co-operate closely with the Spro-cas commissions, particularly those dealing with Politics and Society.

6   Finance

Between 1 February and 31 August 1969, the total expenditure was R8 819,32. The two largest items were salaries for the director and secretary/typist, and travelling costs of members to attend meetings of the commissions.

Revenue received during the period totalled R11 024,15, leaving R2 204,83 unspent. Further contributions are expected in 1970, but if the project is to achieve a significant success it is necessary for considerable further funds to be obtained.

It seems realistic to anticipate that Spro-cas will not finally complete its task before the middle of 1971. In this event a total budget of about R42 000 must be envisaged, of which approximately R7 000 will be needed for an effective publishing and communications programme to be undertaken. Thus, approximately R30 000 will still have to be found. The intention is that this money should be obtained within South Africa, from South African sources.

Peter Randall
30 Sept. 1969

DOCUMENT 3

SPRO-CAS PROGRESS: REPORT TO 2 APRIL 1971

1   Background

The Study Project on Christianity in Apartheid Society comprises six study commissions composed of 150 leading South Africans from many different walks of life. These commissions began to operate in the middle of 1969 and will end their work during 1971 with the publication of comprehensive reports. The six areas of national life being studied are education, economics, politics, law, society and Church. A steering committee consisting of the General Secretary of the South African Council of Churches, the Director of the Christian Institute and the Director of Spro-cas, meets from time to time to determine policy, which a co-ordinating committee drawn from the six commissions assists in reviewing and planning.

The appointment of the Director of Spro-cas has been extended to the 31st of December 1971 in order to see the project to completion. A follow-up programme to implement as far as possible the recommendation of the commissions is envisaged.

2   The Commissions

The Commissions have met regularly during the past two years. Their discussions have been based on working papers (nearly 200 in all) prepared by members of the Commissions or by outside consultants who have included Prof. Nic Rhoodie, Prof. M.H.H. Louw, Chief Gatsha Buthelezi and Prof. W.B. Vosloo.

All the Commissions have now completed their major round of meetings and have appointed drafting committees to prepare their final reports. The first draft of the Education and Church Commissions have been extensively revised in the light of comments from the members of these Commissions. A revised draft of the Education Report has been circulated and it is anticipated that this will be approved, with publication around the end of May. An encouraging feature has been the willingness of drafters to voluntarily give a great deal of time (300 hours in the case of the education drafting Committee) to this task.

3   Publications Programme

Three occasional publications containing selections from the various working papers have been issued *(Anatomy of Apartheid, South Africa's Minorities, Directions of Change in South African Politics)*. All the Spro-cas publications are printed, collated and bound by the staff of the Christian Institute, with a consequent saving in costs. This has made it possible to sell the publications at a low price (50c for the Occasional Publications and R1.00 for the reports).

Demand has exceeded expectations and it will be necessary to reprint the three occasional publications which have already appeared. Altogether 4 127 copies out of 4 487 received from the printing department had been distributed by the 2nd of April. Of these 3 827 had been sold, an increase of 1 250 on the figure for March the 9th.

So far 260 people and institutions have subscribed to the full set of Spro-cas publications, comprising 11 titles in all. Total income from sales of publications at this stage is around R3 500 which in my experience of similar publishing with the South African Institute of Race Relations is very gratifying. Orders have been received from more than 20 countries.

An encouraging feature is the continuing demand for Spro-cas publications from the bookshops, both secular and church. The Rev. D. van Zyl is at present engaged on a countrywide tour to promote the publications and at his first port of call, Potchefstroom, succeeded in obtaining substantial orders from two bookshops.

Reasons for the surprisingly good demand seem to include the good publicity received in the press and in a large variety of journals here and abroad (about 40 in all), and the fact that the writers in the various publications have succeeded in bringing new, important insights into the debate in South Africa on political rights, race relations and social justice.

A fourth occasional publication, *Some Implications of Inequality*, will be issued during April.

The six commissions reports, a co-ordinated Spro-cas report, and the report of the Director of the project will follow during the remainder of 1971. These will be published simultaneously in English and Afrikaans.

4   Future Plans

Obviously the Spro-cas findings and recommendations must be disseminated even more widely if they are to make a significant contribution to thought in South Africa. The project has already evoked valuable responses from one of the major political parties, and the political and economic reports in particular are being awaited with much interest here and abroad. Then we shall have to consider how best to communicate with the general public and how best to translate the findings of the project into action.

Peter Randall
2nd April, 1971

DOCUMENT 4

SOME REACTIONS TO THE SPRO-CAS EDUCATION REPORT

THE REPORT of the Spro-cas Education Commission, *Education beyond Apartheid (Opvoeding Verby Apartheid)*, was published on 9 August 1971. All members of the Spro-cas Commissions were sent a copy of the document, and a summary of some of the reactions to the report may be of interest.

1 Distribution

By the end of November 1971, about 3 250 copies had been distributed, of which 300 were in Afrikaans. Nearly 3 000 copies had been sold, the remainder being review or complimentary copies. Only *Anatomy of Apartheid*, of the first five Spro-cas publications, exceeds this number, 3 552 copies having been distributed by the end of November. (Altogether, nearly 15 000 copies of the five Spro-cas publications had been distributed by this time, for a total income of approximately R10 400 which about broke even with production costs).

A large number of copies of the Education Report went to subscribers to the Spro-cas Publications Programme, who include clergymen, academics, students and educational and other institutions both here and abroad. The S.A. Indian Teachers' Association bought 100 copies for distribution to its branches, the Anglican Church's Education Department took 250 copies for use in its programmes, and a number of study groups and workshops took smaller quantities. The S.A. Institute of Race Relations and the Christian Institute sold considerable numbers through their offices in various centres, and several church and commercial bookshops ordered fairly large quantities. Sympathetic individuals succeeded in selling good quantities at the various church assemblies and synods held between September and November. The Council of Bishops' School ordered a set of the report, and other private schools have shown interest. After the chairman of the commission, Mr Raymond Tunmer, had addressed a meeting of the Transvaal United African Teachers' Association, a steady flow of orders came from African teachers around the province. Some educational institutions, including the Johannesburg College of Education, have placed the report on lists of prescribed or suggested books. The report continues to sell steadily, and indications are that the total number printed in English (4 500) will be distributed over the course of the next year. The 1 500 Afrikaans copies may not be disposed of so readily, and suggestions in this regard will be welcome.

2   Government Response

Advance copies of the report were sent to the Prime Minister, the Ministers of National Education, Bantu Education, Indian Affairs and Coloured Affairs, the directors of Indian and Coloured Education, the Secretary for Bantu Education, and the directors of education in the various provinces. The Prime Minister and several Ministers acknowledged receipt.

The Minister of Bantu Education asked the Department of Bantu Education for comment on the report, and this has been supplied to him by departmental officials in the form of a memorandum. The BED welcomed the fact that the commission's recommendations were made in such a way that those which were capable of implementation in the short term were listed clearly. Many of these are in line with accepted departmental policy and others fit in with future thinking on the part of the department. One of the department's major problems in implementation, it was pointed out, was the lack of adequate finance.

3   Press Coverage

On the release date (9th August) most of the major South African dailies carried reports on *Education beyond Apartheid*. The *Rand Daily Mail* and the *Star* gave the most extensive coverage, which in the case of the former extended over three days. The reporting in the English press was generally factual and stressed the commission's view that wide change was urgently needed in South African education. The *Rand Daily Mail* (11/8/71) followed up its reports with an interview with Major J.D. Opperman, MPC, in which he broadly supported the commission's findings on indoctrination and CNE. In launching its ambitious TEACH campaign ('Teach Every African Child'), the Johannesburg *Star* (7/10/71) drew extensively on the Spro-cas education report.

Die Vaderland avoided any factual report on the Spro-cas Education Commission, but dismissed its work in an editorial (10/8/71) as 'the same tattered old plea for fully integrated education', and the following day published the views of Dr J.C. Otto, M.P., the chairman of the National Party's study group on education. After attacking the commission's 'plea for integration', Dr Otto defended the way in which syllabuses were drawn up, criticised the hypocrisy of English-medium private schools, and accused the

English-speaking of failing to produce enough teachers. *Die Vaderland* concluded that the appearance of the report would actually be 'a great service to the Nationalist government, instead of embarrassing it as was apparently hoped in certain quarters.'

The Cape *Argus* (21/8/71) described the commission's report as 'an explicit document, setting out in detail its plans for a just and Christian education for all.'

4   The Journals

The following journals have given editorial space, reviews or articles to *Education beyond Apartheid* (there may be others of which I am unaware: few editors in this country bother to send copies of reviews etc. to publishers):

> *Dimension* (official journal of the Methodist Church)
> *Pro Veritate* (review by Angela Norman, August 1971)
> *Race Relations News* (review, August 1971)
> *Progress* (review by Dr O.D. Wollheim, Sept. 1971)
> *The Black Sash* (extract, Sept. 1971)
> *Seek* (official journal of the Anglican Church, review, Oct. 71)
> *South African Outlook* (editorial, Sept. 1971)
> *Woord en Daad* (articles: Oct. 1971 and Nov. 1971)
> *Christian Leader* (journal of the Congregational and Presbyterian Churches, Summary, Nov. 1971)
> *The Educational Journal* (organ of the Teachers' League of S.A. -Cape-editorial, Sept. 1971).

Review copies were sent to relevant journals abroad, but so far I have not seen any response.

The *Educational Journal* found the report to be 'pious verbiage' and completely rejected the commission's attempt to work for change from within the apartheid structure. It accused the commission of wishing in fact to preserve 'the essentials of the status quo or, at best, of bringing about gradual, controlled change.'

Woord en Daad described the report as 'important', questioned the fact that non-Christians were invited to serve on the Spro-cas commissions, and said that the commission's plea for the 'inclusive brotherhood of Christ', for the breaking down of religious barriers, for the 'unlimited' freedom of the individual and for a general moral education were 'clear evidence of the liberalistic, humanistic, secularistic life-view which formed the basic motive for the work'. In a second article, *Woord en Daad* challenged the theological assumptions underlying the report, concluding that it revealed a 'sterile neutralism'. The journal will devote a further article to the commission's views on Moral Education.

The *S.A. Outlook* concluded its editorial with the words: 'If a Christian community cannot and will not respond to material of this quality, if they are too indifferent to reach out across denominational barriers and develop a task-force which will study this Report and address itself to implementing at least one of the 49 recommendations of the commission, then indeed that so-called Christian community might just as well cut out its Sunday worship services, revamp the building and flourish as the socio-cultural club that it actually is. Education beyond apartheid is no optional extra. It is one of our very few hopes of achieving peaceful change in South Africa. Only those who care nothing for the future of their children, or have decided to emigrate, can afford to ignore this document and the dire situation to which it bears witness.'

The review in *Seek* summed up the report as 'altogether a stimulating, sensible and thought-provoking report'. The review in *Progress* described it as the 'most forceful and devastating attack upon our present system of education', while *Race Relations News* called it 'a hard-headed analysis ... and a thoughtful and realistic assessment of the need and potential for change ... without being unnecessarily pious about it, the report is firmly grounded in moral convictions'. The review in *Pro Veritate* stressed the value of the recommendations: 'almost any school, educational body or general welfare organisation (e.g. Church women's guild), could find several things they could do immediately'. One of the omissions in the report noted by the reviewer was the lack of adequate space given to adult education, particularly with regard to African women.

5   Follow-up

(i)   As a follow-up to the Education Report, Spro-cas 2 (see memorandum on Special Project for Christian Action in Society) will attempt to develop a meaningful education programme during 1972-73.

(ii)   If the necessary funds can be found, it is proposed to compile and distribute a handbook for private schools, dealing primarily with the question of non-racial admission. This is in response to a specific request from a number of church schools.

(iii)   Contact is being maintained with the Department of Bantu Education and other educational institutions.

Peter Randall
1/12/1971.

DOCUMENT 5

SOME REACTIONS TO THE SOCIAL REPORT

THE REPORT of the Spro-cas Social Commission, *Towards Social Change*, was published on 13 December 1971. Copies were sent to all members of the Spro-cas Commissions, and they may be interested in a summary of some reactions to the report.

1 Distribution

Approximately 3 000 copies of the report have been distributed to date, of which 250 are in Afrikaans. This is somewhat fewer than the number of copies of the Education Report distributed at a comparable stage: one reason may be the fact that the Education Report appealed to a more specific market (teachers societies, students etc). Altogether, nearly 25 000 copies of the eight Spro-cas publications have now been distributed. Of these, the Education Report *(Education beyond Apartheid)* has been most steadily in demand, with 4 300 copies distributed.

Copies of the Social Report were sent to the Prime Minister, relevant Cabinet Ministers and government departments. A large number went to sub-scribers to the Spro-cas publications programme, and many were sold through bookshops, particularly in Johannesburg, Durban and Cape Town. The offices of the Christian Institute, the S.A. Council of Churches, and the S.A. Institute of Race Relations carry stocks and re-order steadily. The reports have been used widely in study groups, both church and secular. The annual conference of the Fraternal Workers of the Tsonga Presbyterian church in February this year took its themes from the Social Report (a memorandum on this conference, including the decisions taken for action, is available from Spro-cas). Prior to the conference a study group within the Church produced an admirable summary of parts of the Report — this was used as the basis for the first Study Aid to be issued by Spro-cas.

2 Press Coverage

The *Star, Die Transvaler,* the *Cape Argus* and the *Natal Daily News* carried factual news reports which concentrated on the final chapter of the report, mentioning the five main goals of social change given there: improvements in the economic position of blacks; closing the gap in average standards of living; a political system without exploitation and control of any group by another group; self-esteem, pride and dignity for all.

The *Sunday Tribune* (19/12/71) carried a lengthy feature article by Brenda Robinson who summarised the main points in the chapters by L. Douwes Dekker, L. Schlemmer and F. van Zyl Slabbert. She said:

> 'Writer after writer slams home the magnitude of the disaster facing South Africa if industrialists, businessmen and employers' associations fail to wake up to the realities of the inadequate wages they pay — and that these men must bear the responsibility'.

The *Sunday Times* (9/1/72) carried a feature article dealing with H. Lever's appendix to the report, which describes apartheid as dishonest rationalisation.

Hoofstad's political correspondent (28/4/72) described his visit to a Cape Town bookshop where books like the Social Report were selling 'like hot cakes' and being 'devoured by young Bantus and white intellectuals'. He contrasted their soft covers, eye-catching designs and cheap prices with the 'handful of books from Afrikaner intellectuals who support separate development', and which are 'not generally available, are expensive and have uninteresting hard covers'. He found *Towards Social Change* to contain 'many statements which would make the Afrikaner's hair rise'. As an example, he quoted the view that many laws and regulations emphasise racial and tribal differences among blacks, hence undermining any sense of a shared position of being discriminated against.

He concluded:

> 'The lesson is very clear. If the Afrikaners do not quickly wake up and fight the integrationists, even with their own weapons, separate development may lose the battle in the last ditch, the cities.'

3   The Journals

Southern Cross, official journal of the Catholic Church, carried a review (26/4/72) which described the report as 'highly competent, well documented and written by experts ... a mine of information ... The facts given in it, so unemotionally, are a sufficiently devastating exposure ... 'The reviewer felt that 'in all movements an intellectual core is needed', a simpler approach should be adopted for 'Everyman' (see earlier note on Study Aid).

Africa Acts Feature Service of Nairobi disseminated an article by Norman

Hart, which consisted mainly of a summary of the points made in Schlemmer's chapter on Strategies for Change. He felt that none of the Spro-cas reports 'will arouse more comment in South Africa and outside', and concluded that 'the question is will black people hear what this report has to say and are they ready to act on it ?' The article was reproduced in full by *Pro Veritate* in its May, 1972, issue.

A 'prominent Anglican layman' reviewed the report in the March, 1972, issue of *Seek*, the official journal of the Anglican Church, under the heading 'Just not good enough'. The reviewer accused the report of throwing 'a blanket on misguided people like the Liberals' and of 'actively discouraging Church members who are doing their best'. He felt that Spro-cas should rather 'sound a trumpet which will gather all active Christians together, ready to face the foe'. A reply to this review by the director of Spro-cas appeared in the April issue, pointing out that the report actually indicates an encouraging variety of potential methods of change and that change demands more than 'the tired blowing of trumpets'.

In its issues of May, 1972, *Reality* carried a lengthy critique of the Social Report ('A Tragic Report') by Mrs Fatima Meer, who was a member of the Commission but did not sign the report. Mrs Meer concluded her critique with the words 'It seems quite apparent that the 'new liberals' are so overawed by the power of the present government, and so fearful of losing white sympathy, that they dare not propose change, and thus this tragic report.' One of her major criticisms was that the Report did not pay sufficient attention to franchise proposals.

A reply by L. Schlemmer, secretary to the Commission, was published by *Reality* in June, saying that 'it requires no great insight to realise that blacks in South Africa need the vote', and that 'the Report states quite clearly that a universal franchise could probably be effective in safeguarding justice in South Africa .... universal franchise would be an essential but possibly not a sufficient condition for safeguarding justice .... '

Mr Schlemmer questioned a number of other assumptions which underlay Mrs Meer's critique.

The newsletter of the *Civil Rights League* (28/2/72): 'Change is in the air in South Africa .... for those who wish to bring it down to earth we commend wholeheartedly the Spro-cas publication, *Towards Social Change.*'

A review in Race Relations News (Feb. 1972) concluded 'there is something here of value for everyone concerned about understanding South African society and about working for change in that society .... (it) will obviously make a major contribution to the strategies and methods that Spro-cas 2 will adopt.' (Spro-cas 2 is the Special Project for Christian Action in Society, which follows on from the work of the Spro-cas I study commissions).

The *Black Sash* journal (March 1972) reprinted an extract from the chapter by M.G. Whisson on the white liberal groups. It introduced this by saying: 'The Spro-cas reports are essential reading for members of any organisation which hopes and works for change towards a just society in South Africa.'

Progress (Jan. 1972) quoted the abstract of the Report, and a number of other journals carried brief notices about the report.

South African Outlook (Jan. 1972) described the report as 'a very sound piece of work .... impresses by its lack of liberal illusions .... perhaps (its) greatest value is the practical guidelines it furnishes for fighting racism.'

Peter Randall
20/6/72.

DOCUMENT 6

SOME REACTIONS TO THE CHURCH REPORT

THE REPORT of the Spro-cas Church Commission, *Apartheid and the Church*, was published at the beginning of August, 1972. Copies were sent to all members of the Spro-cas Commissions, for whom the following summary of reactions is primarily intended.

1   Distribution

Approximately 2 800 copies of the report have been distributed to date, which compares very favourably with the three previous Spro-cas reports. The figures for the other reports are as follows:

Education beyond Apartheid (pub. August 1971)	5 000 copies
Towards Social Change (pub. December 1971)	3 750 copies
Power, Privilege and Poverty (pub. June 1972)	3 150 copies

Only the Education and Social reports are presently available in Afrikaans. Translations are, however, being prepared of the Church and Economics reports.

Copies of the Church Report were sent to the Prime Minister and the Minister of the Interior (from whom no acknowledgements were received), to the leaders of the various Christian denominations in South Africa, and to student leaders at the various seminaries. Several responses were received from Church leaders, particularly Anglican bishops. The Bishop of Kimberley and Kuruman wrote that 'the Report will be specially helpful to those who will be serving on our Challenge Group and other related groups in the Diocese'. The Suffragan Bishop of Johannesburg wrote that 'many of the Recommendations are in line with our Programme for Human Relations and Reconciliation', and offered to do what he could to commend the Report.

Other Anglican leaders, like the Bishop of Natal, commended the report at Synods and in press statements.

The only formal response from the Roman Catholic leadership came from Cardinal McCann, who wrote to say that he was referring the report to the Administrative Board of the Episcopal Conference.

Very little feedback has been received of the use made of the Church Report at the various Church Synods, Assemblies and Conferences held since it was published.

2   Press Coverage

Both the *Sunday Tribune* and the *Sunday Times* (6th August 1972) gave factual reports, with a summary of the subject content, a list of the signatories and some of the recommendations. Highlighted in separate articles in both newspapers was the argument over the suitability of the cover, this included pictures.

The *Cape Argus* of the 8th October carried a summarised report in point form, with their pick of the signatories. On the 9th October it carried an editorial in which it called it 'an appeal which should embrace more than the church going members of the community ... If this is the Christian spirit, the answer is clear to any mind unclouded by ideological prejudice. It is the only way for racial and national unity!'

The *Star* (9th August) carried a brief account of the contents of the report. The *Rand Daily Mail* (10th August) report referred to the covering note which 'gave evidence of the state's interference with the rights of the clergy to proclaim the gospel'.

On the 11th it carried a report on comments of various church representatives. This included the comment of Rev. E.S. Pons of the Presbyterian Church of South Africa that 'the Spro-cas call was nothing contrary to what we have always advocated', and the comment of a spokesman for Bishop Boyle, of the Roman Catholic Church, 'All ministers irrespective of colour received the same remuneration. Discussions have been initiated in all parishes to remove all forms of racialism from the church'. Rev. H.C. Snyders of the NGK refused to comment.

The *Cape Times* report of 10th August described the report as being critical of both the Church and the norms of the South African society which influenced it. It also listed the proposals. On the 21st the Cape Times also gave a full and lengthy report of the book's contents.

The *Pretoria News* of the 10th August carried both an article and an editorial. The article was full and factual and the editorial stated that 'the Spro-cas Commission has given all South Africans much to think about at a time when such matters are increasingly burdening the consciences of many. It has added what may be the crucial material to a ferment of thought from which new South African attitudes promise to emerge.'

The article in *Rapport* of the 13th August was mostly factual but highlighted the point that 'the Dutch Reformed Church is better than the English churches, which by their own admission are hypocritical', and used the facts of the report to attack them.

3   Journals

The *Southern Cross* of the 16th August gave a full page factual and analytical account of the book, which dealt with the covering letter, the effects of apartheid and denominationalism and gave the recommendations. The journal commented: 'We Catholics have our own history of pronouncements condemning racial prejudices and discrimination, at the same time should observe the credibility gap in our actual practice .... 'Apartheid and the Church' can help us face up to the credibility gap and to see some practical steps towards a sincere Christian life.

We need to take seriously the point that heresy in action needs to be as clearly denounced as heresy in doctrine. The churches .... should be persuaded to draw up confessions of faith .... which state clearly their position on the racial issue, if possible .... together.'

This journal gave the Church report the fullest coverage.

Kairos (August) of the South African Council of Churches said 'Whatever people may think of the cover, the report itself is a challenging document. If it hurts at certain points we hope that it will also lead to healing.'

Dimension, 3rd September said that despite the cover 'the real attention getter is likely to be the content of the report, which spells out the many ways in which the Church in South Africa is hindered .... by the complexities of Apartheid legislation.' *Dimension* also carried a full page analysis which included the recommendations. (1st October, 1972).

Pro Veritate (15 October) in an article by Professor Ben Marais devoted their book review column to the Church report and referred to it as: 'really excellent, stimulating and penetrating. The argumentation is precise and the facts marshalled generally to the point. Every page is challenging .... It is written against the broad background of the ecumenical and missionary thinking of our day and as such is truly up to date .... It avoids all the pitfalls by clearly distinguishing between concepts.'

Seek (October) carried an article written by the Rt. Rev. John Carter, Bishop Suffragan of Johannesburg, in which he said 'It is just because many of us do try to escape thinking about apartheid and its power to diminish humanity that we ought to buy this book, get beyond the cover, and face up to the meaning of renewal ... Here is the stuff for Christians who are not afraid of the truth — or of the cost of obedience.'

New Nation (October) carried a short analysis and critique in which it stated that the discussion of one point was inadequate for 'it leaves the reader with an important question unanswered. No clear line between institutional involvement of the church in social and political matters and Christian involvement is drawn.' It then went on to say: 'As a whole the report carried a serious message to black and white churches alike and it does not fail to have a disconcerting effect on the lay reader through its uncovering of the tacit alliance of the white Christian with an ideology which is described as non-scriptural, even heretical.'

> 'As a whole the report carried a serious message to Black and White Churches alike and it does not fail to have a disconcerting effect on the lay reader through its uncovering of the tacit alliance of the White Christian with an ideology which is described as non-scriptural, even heretical.'

Dimension in a later issue carried an editorial on the Church report in which it dealt with the implications for the Methodist Church which had 'particular dishonourable mention' in this 'urgent document which demands deep and honest searching in relation to all levels of its church's life .... This report reminds us strongly not only that recommendations and reports are but words which need translation into actions, but also that the real task lies in the redemption of attitudes and motives ... This report reminds us, too, that it is already so very very late.'

Marie-Jeanne Wytenburg
16/11/1972

DOCUMENT 7

SPRO-CAS 2: MEMORANDUM

TENTATIVE PROPOSALS for a follow-up action programme to the Study Project on Christianity in Apartheid Society (sponsored jointly by the South African Council of Churches and the Christian Institute of Southern Africa, 1969 - 1971).

NOTE:

This is only a preliminary draft, which will be reconsidered when the reports of the six Spro-cas Commissions (economics, education, law, politics, society and the church) become available later in 1971. Mr L. Schlemmer, Deputy Director of the Institute for Social Research, Natal University, and Secretary of the Spro-cas Social Commission will also be submitting detailed proposals which will be incorporated at a later stage.

1   Time Scale

It is suggested that 'Spro-cas Two' commence at the beginning of 1972 and be regarded initially as a two year project with the position to be reviewed in mid-1973.

2   Context

In 1968 the Theological Commission of the South African Council of Churches published the Message to the People of South Africa, a theological critique of apartheid. It was to study the implications of the Message for our national life that Spro-cas was established. The Spro-cas Commissions will be making far-reaching proposals for change in the direction of a just, non-discriminatory society in South Africa.

'Spro-cas Two' is thus a logical further step in a major and sustained attempt to achieve change in Southern Africa, involving the talents and hard work of many South Africans (150 are serving on the six study commissions).

The sequence can be shown as:

(i)   The theological study resulting in the Message which stimulated
(ii) the intellectual study of the Spro-cas commissions,
(iii) the action programme of 'Spro-cas Two'.

'Spro-cas Two' can be seen as the final phase of a three phase programme aimed at achieving social change and social justice in South Africa.

3   Broad Aims of 'Spro-cas Two'

(i)   To implement as far as possible those immediately practicable recommendations for change made by the six Spro-cas Study Commissions.
(ii) To prepare the ground for the eventual implementations of the long-term recommendations for change made by the six Spro-cas Study Commissions.
(iii) To undertake further action in line with the findings of the Spro-cas Study Commissions.

4   Basic Material

(i)   The reports, publications and working documents of Spro-cas.
(ii) Relevant literature from other countries relating to social change, etc.

A number of Spro-cas documents are particularly relevant in deciding on strategies: the following are a few of these:

(i)   *Practical Programme to reduce Inter-Group Tensions:*
       Prof. H. Lever
(ii)   *Cultural Diversity and Politics in South Africa:*
       Dr J. van Zyl Slabbert
(iii) *Social Organisations ... and ...: Change:*
       Dr M.G. Whisson
(iv)   *Programme for Change through the Institutional Network:*
       Mr L. Douwes Dekker
(v)   *Strategies for Change:*
       Mr L. Schlemmer
(vi)   *Education and Social Change:*
       Mr M.J. Ashley

(vii) *Effective Participation in Government:*
Mr A.B. du Toit
(viii) *The Significance of Local Government in a Plural Society:*
Mrs N.J. Charton
(ix) *Some Aspects of Culture and Apartheid:*
Mr. André Brink (published in *Anatomy of Apartheid* — Spro-cas Publication No. 1).

The tentative proposals for 'Spro-cas Two' which follow are to some extent based on the thinking in these and other papers, but a careful study must be made in order to devise a well thought-out and detailed programme of action. It is suggested in the latter part of 1971 a small group of about 12 - 18 experts drawn from the Spro-cas Study commissions should be called together to undertake this pre-planning for 'Spro-cas Two'. Possible members of such a group could be Mr L. Schlemmer, Dr F. Wilson, Mr M. Fransman, Rev D. van Zyl, Rev D. Poynton, Archbishop Denis Hurley, Dr F. van Zyl Slabbert, Prof A.P. Hunter, Prof J. Dugard, Dr R. Turner, Mr John Rees, the Rev Beyers Naudé, Dr A. Boraine, Bishop B.B. Burnett, Prof W.M. Kgware, Fr C.B. Collins, Mr J. Moloto, Mr A.B. du Toit, Prof A.S. Mathews, Dr D. Welsh, Mr M.T. Moerane. This group would have only a limited life span in order to formulate clear goals, priorities and strategies for 'Spro-cas Two'. It could also, however, form the nucleus of a co-ordinating committee for 'Spro-cas Two'.

5 Tentative Structure

See Diagram on Page 164

6 Sponsors

The Christian Institute of Southern Africa and possibly other bodies. The degree of likely co-operation of the South African Council of Churches is not at present clear.

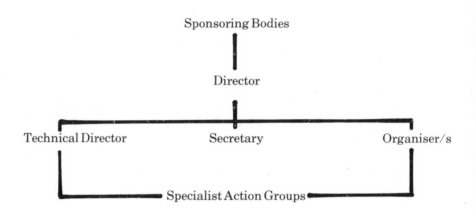

Sponsoring Bodies

Director

Technical Director   Secretary   Organiser/s

Specialist Action Groups

The Action Groups would be specifically oriented to work in separate fields:
Economics, Culture, Church, Education etc.

Co-ordinating Committee

Communications Committee

Clerical and other Staff

7 Staff

(i) *Director:* To be responsible for overall policy, co-ordination and administration, in conjunction with the Steering Committee.

(ii) *Organiser:* To be responsible for the organisation of meetings of the action groups, and conferences, seminars, workshops and courses in conjunction with the Action Groups and the Steering Committee. With the Director, to implement the projects and programmes formulated by the Action Groups.

(iii) *Technical Director:* To be responsible for the publishing programme in conjunction with the Action Groups and the Steering Committee. To undertake the preparation and production of such printed materials as required for seminars, workshops and training courses in conjunction with other staff. To advise on all technical matters relating to administration etc.

    The aims to establish a compact, flexible and skilled team commanding a variety of resources, contacts and abilities which can be pooled. The emphasis must be on organisational and practical ability as much as on academic qualification and intellectual insights. The three executives would work in the closest co-operation and jointly staff the Action Groups. A possibility to be considered is that the organiser might be based in Durban or Cape Town with other executives in Johannesburg. This would have to be decided in the light, *inter alia*, of the geographic distribution of the Action Groups.

(iv) *Clerical Staff:* A minimum of four clerical and general office staff would be required for the envisaged programmes. Again, a variety of skills is important.

8 Steering Committee

Composed of representatives of the sponsors and the executive staff of 'Spro-cas Two'. To meet from time to time to review progress and determine policy.

9   Co-ordinating Committee

Drawn from the different Action Groups and staffed by the senior executives. To meet from time to time to exchange information and ideas, coordinate efforts, and discuss future plans. This Committee should be compact, able to meet at short notice in different parts of the country, and its members should be strongly committed to work actively for change.

10   Communications Committee

Drawn from the Action Groups with additional outside experts in the various media, and working primarily with the Technical Director. Such a Committee would play a vital role in the dissemination and propagation of the work of 'Spro-cas Two'. Much of the success to date of the Spro-cas publications programme has been due to thorough groundwork and planning (the initial printing of the first three titles has been sold out in less than 6 months). The voluntary assistance of design experts and journalists can be counted on.

11   The Action Groups

These are divided fairly arbitrarily at present, and a completely different division into areas of action may emerge at a later stage.

The detailed programmes of action to be undertaken can be formulated only after considerable further thought and discussion and after all the Sprocas reports have been issued. Useful guidelines have already been given, however, in the 200 working papers prepared for the Study Commissions, particularly the papers by Mr L. Schlemmer, Mr L. Douwes Dekker and Prof. H. Lever (already listed) from which some of the following preliminary suggestions have been taken. Study of those areas which are vulnerable to change in South Africa has been part of the task of the commissions, and a realistic assessment of actions which are feasible and likely to be effective is now correspondingly easier (see, for example, 'The Present Political Postition' and 'Factors Underlying Apartheid in *Anatomy of Apartheid* — Spro-cas Publication No. 1; and 'Thoughts on the Common Society' by Alan Paton, and 'Implications of recent Policies' by L. Schlemmer in *Directions of Change in South African Politics* — Spro-cas Publication No. 3; also the papers listed previously). In such fields as black community development, white attitudinal change, 'cultural confrontation', economic processes affecting change, issues like non-racial sport, the potential role of foreign investors in South Africa etc., the respective Action Groups would have to assign priorities and determine effective strategies on the basis of material already produced by the Spro-cas Commissions, and on-going research and study (two Spro-cas Commissioners, for example, are at present engaged in a pilot survey of the attitudes of urbanised Afrikaners in Durban and if the necessary funds are forthcoming this survey will be extended to other cities).

12 Possible Action - Projects

(Specific recommendations made by the different Spro-cas Commissions will be incorporated later).

(i)   *An educational programme* along the lines of the 'Springfield Plan' in the U.S.A., aimed initially at the church schools (for details see Lever p. 2 - 4). Close co-operation would have to be established with the programmes of the South African Institute of Race Relations and the youth and Education Departments of those churches which have embarked on similar projects.

(ii)   *Community self-surveys* aimed at both action and research. The verified assumption is that motivation will be high as a result of participating in the fact-finding process and that the experience gained by using the scientific method is a good preparation for the programme of action that the community will decide upon. The community self-survey can be used to good effect, for example, in combatting discriminatory practices in employment and in health and poverty programmes. (Lever p. 10 - 12).

(iii) *Collective Credit Schemes* might be one outcome of (ii) whereby communities are assisted in regular, planned savings in order to make more effective use of low incomes for e.g. by avoiding hire purchase and building up capital for self-help projects.

(iv)   *Post-literacy Training* might be another, whereby newly literate people are provided with suitable literature, for example on elementary budgeting, nutrition, farming techniques, etc.

(v)   *An Economic Action Programme* might include, for example:
(a)   action directed at South Africa and foreign companies to pay better wages, provide more social security etc. for black workers (see Randall: *To Engage or not to Engage*, Pro Veritate, May 1971, for specific suggestions);
(b)   action with regard to the establishment of worker's committees;

(c) the compilation and dissemination of a code of ethics regarding institutional behaviour (see Douwes Dekker p. 24);
(d) disseminating to employers and employers organisations
results of research on the relationship between poverty and under-
productivity, and experiments in the advancement of non-whites;
(e) a concerted drive to publicise the extent of poverty and lack of
opportunity in South Africa;
(f) assistance in establishing rural co-operatives for Africans.

(vi) *Changing White Attitudes:* Intensive efforts directed at opinion
leaders from various groups and strata, along the lines suggested
by Schlemmer (Strategies for change p. 6 - 7).

(vii) *Utilising the Mass Media*, involving, for example:
(a) research into typical reactions to various types of socio-
political reporting;
(b) a series of popular and easily understood yet authoritative
articles predicting the outcome of various changes;
(c) skillfully conducted opinion polls, which in themselves tend
to facilitate shifts in political opinion;
(d) dramatic, popular ways of illustrating inter-dependence of
the races.

There is considerable scope for using the mass media in South
Africa in a more systematic, deliberate and focussed way (for
further details see Schlemmer p. 7 - 9).

(viii) *Efforts to counteract black powerlessness* (see suggestions in
Schlemmer p. 17ff).

(ix) *Publications Programme:* This would arise organically from the
work of the Action Groups. Other possibilities include a regular
journal on change and strategies for change (possibly entitled
'Towards Social Change'), post-literacy material, supplementary
teaching material, 'study kits', and collaboration with existing
journals like *Pro Veritate*. It must be stressed again that the
above does not represent a systematic and comprehensive programme, but merely indicates some of the proposals on which the
detailed programme of the Action Groups of 'Spro-cas Two' will be
based.

Other projects might include a political programme to propagate alternative policies; work for the formation of a non-racial teachers' society and other institutional associations.

In summary, 'Spro-cas Two' will aim to facilitate the type of change, enunciated by Mr Schlemmer, which will ultimately:

(a)   lead to steady improvements in the economic position of the majority of non-whites;

(b)   have the effect of closing the gap in average standards of living between non-white and white groups;

(c)   result in steady improvements in regard to the civil liberties, social benefits, and freedom under the law enjoyed by members of all groups in the population of South Africa;

(d)   lead to political arrangement in South Africa which will avoid the exploitation and control of any one group by another group;

(e)   allow all members of all groups to enjoy self-esteem, pride, dignity and a release from those factors which presently undermine the morale and self-respect of individual members of non-white groups, as well as an elimination of factors which under-mine the social health of whole communities, particularly the poorer ones.

Peter Randall
9 September 1971

DOCUMENT 8

BLACK COMMUNITY PROGRAMMES

Tentative Suggestions for Action

Objectives

The goals of Spro-cas 2 are spelt out clearly in the document prepared by the Director in June 1971.

(i)   'To implement as far as possible those immediately practicable recommendations for change made by the six Spro-cas Study Commissions.
(ii) To prepare the ground for the eventual implementations of the long-term recommendations for change made by the six Study Commissions.
(iii) To undertake further action in line with the findings of Spro-cas Study Commissions.'

Specifically, the goals of the Black Community Programmes of Spro-cas 2 are:

(i)   To help the Black Community become aware of its own identity.
(ii) To help the Black Community to create a sense of its own power.
(iii) To enable the Black Community to organise itself, to analyse its own needs and problems and to mobilise its resources to meet its needs.
(iv) To develop black leadership capable of guiding the development of black communities.

What will it take to get the Programme Moving?

Spro-cas 2 presupposes an urgency in our situation that will not wait for anyone. If we do not become genuinely connected to the 'gut-issues' of our life here, we risk extinction even before we move a leg.

Spro-cas 2 needs to hook-up with forces in the community working for social change and responding to the needs that these communities disclose.

This movement toward involvement will require vital shifts in emphasis from the 'traditional' ways of dealing with community problems.

The following continuum suggests in outline the dimensions these shifts in emphasis must take as we participate 'responsively' in the transformation of the Black Communities. I will amplify the intent of each shift.

From: *Service ... to ... Action*

From serving the individual needs of people to action to build a power base for systematic reform in the community.

From: *Symptoms ... to ... Causes*

From dealing with symptoms to dealing with causes.

From: *Working Alone ... to ... Working with Others*

From working alone to working with others to develop an overall strategy, that is, working with other community action groups, grassroots community groups, churches etc.

From: *Responsible People ... to ... Responsive People*

From people who move with constant caution to people who are responsive to community needs. The desire for 'responsible' activity is often a cover for doing nothing at all.

From: *Diffusion ... to ... Power*

From offering a little bit of everything towards a reordering of resources behind specific goals.

From: *Doing for the Poor ... to ... Working with and Under*

From doing things for people to working with people, helping them to discover their needs and helping them organise their programme.

From: *Whitemen Working in Black Communities*
                                    ... to ...
                Blackmen Working in Black Communities

From white-staffed programmes for blacks toward predominantly black-staffed programmes for black people. The hardest job remains. Whites must learn to work for change in the white community; the missionary area for white people is not in the black communities, but the white communities.

1   From Service to Action

In past efforts, insofar as we sought to change society, we sought to change it through the transformation of the individuals that composed it. Yet it is increasingly apparent that our concentration on individual and inter-personal relationships and efforts to reform the wayward and to relieve problems of the 'disadvantaged' has been inadequate and superficial. The problem we face is not simply that of individual bigotry. The racial crisis is not caused simply as a result of the sum total of everyone's individual prejudice. We are now becoming aware of the ways in which the whole white institutional life functions subtly but effectively to prevent blacks from genuine participation in the economic, educational, Church and political structures of the country.

Our programmes therefore are called upon to be more than 'remedial'. We must embark on efforts to build among those with whom we choose to work, the means to achieve, and opportunities for using power — political and social. In addition we must assist efforts in white suburban areas towards the same end. They too are largely ignorant of the political process and the role they can play in it. Unlike black communities however, they have 'protectors' whose interests are more like their own.

2.   From Symptoms to Causes

Some people have distinguished between 'problems' and 'issues'. When one man cannot get along with his wife, that's a problem. When three men out of ten don't get along with their wives, that's an 'issue'. It's not just a matter of degree. The focus is changed from 'what's wrong with him?' to 'what's wrong with US?'.

Spro-cas 2 must address itself to the causes of the social ills and other 'disadvantages' of the black community. To do this we need to get involved in the struggle for quality education, health care, public housing and the myriad other points at which members of the black community are affected.

3   From working alone to working with others to develop an overall strategy

To change our society, we must ally ourselves with those in the community who are now the vanguard of social change.

Our crisis will not be resolved until an overall strategy is developed which combines the major segments of our society:- Business, Government,

Churches, Labour and non-governmental agencies like our own. Only a combination of forces can solve the interrelated problems of white institutional racism.

4   From Diffusion to Power

No one can say with certainty what another community or person really needs. but one can come closest by knowing people in the community itself. Staff people particularly need to be in touch on many levels — with people in present programmes, colleagues in related fields, local leaders (both established and grassroots) as well as people presently unrelated to community organisations where programmes might be made available.

An agency that seeks to do everything suggested to it betrays an underlying rootlessness and lack of direction. We should seek to do that which we consider most urgent and that which we have the resources to meet. We can determine priorities on the basis of community needs and then, by reviewing present programmes, determine which programmes are relevant.

5   From doing for the poor to working with and under

The greatest danger facing any agency today is the temptation to do programmes for 'poor' people and for 'black people' without involving them centrally in the planning and execution. We must find ways of ending the parternalistic effect of this practice.

We must instead determine ways in which those whites who are interested can supply resources and technical assistance which black people need to develop programmes in their own communities.

6   From Whitemen Working in Black Communities to Blackmen working in Black Communities.

Race is important. The Churches, as well as other 'liberal' agencies dedicated to the achieving of an integrated society, sought to destroy or ignore distinctions between black and white (they sought to be colour-blind rather than colour-sensitive). They said to themselves and others 'colour is not important .... it's the man within'. They pretended even to themselves not to see the differences in man's skin. But it didn't work. It did and does matter to both. It matters very much. This is what Black Consciousness is all about, and until this is recognized these agencies cannot move beyond it.

We are increasingly aware of the largely negative impact whites have in the black community. Certain programmes have turned from placing whites in the black community to actively recruiting more blacks for that work. We now see that much of their work, done with the best of intentions, has often perpetuated a sense of dependency and paternalism.

What we would like to see through these programmes is blacks working constructively on the 'black problem' of jobs, education, housing, welfare etc, while whites learn to confront white people and white institutions in white communities with the 'white problem'.

METHODS

In putting these into effect, there are at least two possible methods of approach:

The first is that Spro-cas can set out to establish projects such as 'self-help' agencies in the black communities to do the work along the line outlined in the body of this document.

If this approach is followed we would require a staff and financial outlay which would exceed the present means of Spro-cas 2. Also, setting up new projects may tend to duplicate existing efforts, perhaps to the detriment of the designs of the programme as set out here.

The second method is the one I prefer. This approach seeks to *communicate, co-ordinate,* and *co-operate* in a meaningful way with other groups, organisations and institutions — both public and private, in the black communities, to enable them to make the necessary shifts in programme emphasis so that they can create a consciousness of identity as communities, develop sufficient individuals conscious of this identity and belonging and ability to acquire and use resources needed to achieve the goals of unity, self-determination, collective work responsibility, purpose and creativity.

The rationale for this kind of approach is that there are in already existing organisations — welfare, education, recreation, church etc. — 'Change Agents' (Leaders) working in these organisations; what these agents require are skills, information and techniques to improve communication, and understanding of the goals of their organisations. Our aim should be to see to what extent we can help them to be more effective in their own setting — in a sense, to train them to become better 'change agents'.

In this approach stress is laid on the need to encourage communities to identify their wants and needs and to work co-operatively at satisfying them. In this approach 'projects' are not determined but develop as discussion in communities focusses the real concerns of the people. As needs and wants are defined and solutions sought we in Spro-cas may provide the kind of aid which assists the community in meeting these needs. But, the emphasis is on communities working at their own problems. Change comes as a community sees the need for change and as it develops the will and capacity to make changes it sees as desirable.

Our aim should be to heighten this will and capacity to make changes that are desirable. Direction is then established internally rather than externally. The development of a specific project is less imprtant than the development of the capacity of a people to establish the project.

The Churches in this country have indicated, by sponsoring the Spro-cas programme and other programmes, their desire to be involved in the task of eradicating all those factors that contribute to the 'powerlessness' of the black communities, and it is hoped that as these programmes start the individual churches are going to put their resources and good offices open to the implementation of most of the programmes. Close liaison will be kept with Christian Education Departments of churches as well as other key persons working on church programmes.

LIMITATIONS

The main limitations of the above approach are: (i) Action will be slow; (ii) The action taken is not subject to control by us; (iii) The programmes that develop may not be the action which we feel we necessarily agree with, and the action taken may move in 'unsophisticated' fashion.

On the other hand we must emphasise the importance of people learning to work together at the problems *they* conceive to be important, and the probability that such projects as the community undertakes in this fashion will have a meaning and permanence which imposed projects, no matter how subtly introduced, will not have.

COST AND PERSONNEL

To undertake such programmes a Director of the Programmes is obviously necessary. His task will be to organise and give direction to the goals of the programme. Much of his time will be taken by travelling and speaking to groups and individuals as well as setting up such workshops, seminars and conferences as are necessary.

It would appear that a Field Officer whose main tasks would be to collect data about communities as well as keeping contact with points of development will be necessary if the budget can carry such a person.

It also becomes evident that in order to improve and maintain good communication with black communities there will be a need for at least a simple publication to carry news about the black communities as well as the work of other black organisations in the country on a regular basis.

All these things have an implication for the budget available for the two year period.

CONCLUSION

In this outline I have made tentative suggestions only and for obvious reasons I have not set out to answer problems or make firm predictions. Detailed proposals will be made as the work begins to unfold. I have merely tried to set out what directions this programme should take as I see it at this stage.

B.A. Khoapa
Durban 30 September 1971

DOCUMENT 9

SPRO-CAS 2: MEMORANDUM DATED 23/12/71

1 Basic Principles and Aims

(i) Spro-cas 2 will seek to make a positive contribution to the creation of a better social order in South Africa, one based on Christian values such as justice, freedom and equality of opportunity.

(ii) The study commissions of Spro-cas 1 (the Study Project on Christianity in Apartheid Society) have analysed our society and shown where change is both feasible and most urgently needed. In seeking change in our society, we shall:
(a) implement as far as possible those immediately practicable recommendations for change made by the six Spro-cas study commissions, and
(b) concentrate all available resources on the most effective areas in which work can be undertaken to bring about movement towards a more Christian society.

2 Basic Approach

We recognise that the present South African society is deeply divided, and this implies that in seeking to bring about change our resources need to be used in a dual thrust into both the black and white communities. Spro-cas 2 will thus aim to develop programmes relevant to the differing needs of black and white that will facilitate the achievement of a better social order in South Africa.

3 Time Scale

Spro-cas 2 is initially regarded as a two-year project, starting 1 January 1972, with the position to be reviewed in mid-1973.

4   Planning

The planning for Spro-cas 2 has extended over the latter part of 1971. Informal discussions were held with a large number of individuals and organisations, culminating in a meeting of twenty five people in Johannesburg in October 1971, under the chairmanship of Archbishop Denis Hurley. Among those present were representatives from the different Spro-cas study commissions and people from a variety of relevant organisations, including ASSECA, NUSAS, the South African Institute of Race Relations, the South African Council of Churches, the Christian Institute and labour relations organisations.

The present memorandum was then drawn up by the prospective staff of Spro-cas 2, in consultation with the South African Council of Churches and the Christian Institute of Southern Africa.

5   Sponsors

The joint sponsors of Spro-cas 2 are the South African Council of Churches and the Christian Institute of Southern Africa, who were the sponsors of Spro-cas 1.

6   Programmes

In broad summary Spro-cas 2 will aim in its strategy to be
- (a)   an *enabling* body, seeking out action already occurring, and stimulating new action;
- (b)   a *participant* as far as possible in the on-going institutional network in the country;
- (c)   a *decentralised* body, working through local groups and responding to local issues, as well as having a centralised function in terms of national interests and national issues.

Implementation of the Programmes
Four major areas of action have tentatively been decided upon:
Education
Economics
Church
Social Issues

It is important that the actual programmes to be undertaken in these areas should grow out of the needs of people themselves, rather than be pre-determined beforehand. The staff of Spro-cas 2 will be helped in formulation of relevant programmes by Consultative Panels in the four areas listed above. The approach must be a dynamic one, allowing for change in methods as situations and circumstances change. In other words, action will be both preceded and succeeded by reflection. The dual thrust outlined in para. 2 will be reflected in black programmes and white programmes, which will draw on a common pool of resources. Since the needs of the black community and the white community are not the same, it would be futile to attempt identical programmes in each community.

7   Publications Programme

    (i)   In the first place this involves the completion of the publishing programme of Spro-cas 1, i.e. the reports of the study commissions and the co-ordinated Spro-cas Report.

   (ii)   As at present, the publishing of Spro-cas Literature will be undertaken in conjunction with the Christian Institute, which possesses the necessary equipment.

8   Research

Allowance is made in the proposed budget for ad hoc research into relevant topics, so that where further information is needed on which to base meaningful action it can be provided.

9   The Consultative Panels

It is necessary to have a balance between those who are essentially thinkers and those who are essentially activists. The consultative panels will be regionally based, with smaller groups meeting in Durban and Johannesburg to assist staff in planning and implementation as needed. The members of the panels will be drawn partly from the Spro-cas study commissions, with the addition of new people with relevant experience and expertise in the four fields of operation.

10   Co-ordinating Committee

A co-ordinating committee drawn from the different panels and local groups and executive staff will meet from time to time to exchange information and ideas, co-ordinate efforts and discuss future plans.

The aim for this committee will be that it should be compact, able to meet at short notice in different parts of the country if necessary, and that its members should be strongly committed to work for change.

11   Communications Committee

Composed of experts in the various media, this committee will be available for consultation by the Communications Director, and will play a vital role in the dissemination and propagation of the work of Spro-cas 2.

12   Steering Committee

Composed of representatives of the Sponsors and the executive staff of Spro-cas 2, the Steering Committee will meet from time to time to review progress and determine policy. Close liaison with the sponsoring bodies will be maintained.

13   Staff

(i)   *Director:* To be responsible for overall policy, co-ordination and administration, in conjunction with the Steering Committee. Based in Johannesburg.
     Mr Peter Randall has been appointed director of Spro-cas 2. He is a former teacher and lecturer, was assistant director of the South African Institute of Race Relations from 1965 to 1969, and has directed Spro-cas 1 from its inception.

(ii)   *Director of Black Community Programmes:* To organise and give direction to the goals of the programmes. Much of his time will be taken in travelling and speaking to groups and individuals as well as setting up such workshops, seminars and conferences as are necessary. Based in Durban.
     Mr Bennie A. Khoapa has accepted this post. Mr Khoapa graduated as a Social Worker in 1959 and after working as a personnel welfare officer

was appointed Secretary for African work of the South African National Council of Y.M.C.A.'s in 1964. He held this position until the end of 1971. During this period he undertook a special course of training in the U.S.A.

(iii) *Communications Director:* To be responsible for the publishing programme and to undertake the preparation and production of material required for seminars, workshops and training courses, in conjunction with other staff. To advise on all technical matters relating to administration, and to explore the use of media such as records and films. Based in Johannesburg.

The Rev Danie van Zyl has accepted this appointment. He is a minister of the Tsonga Presbyterian Church and formerly worked for the South African Institute of Race Relations. He was the Christian Institute's Adviser to AICA and Programme Director of the Theological Correspondence Courses of AICA (the African Independent Churches Association) after completing a course in Educational Psychology and Technology at Birmingham University. He has also worked very closely with Spro-cas 1, particularly in the publishing programme.

(iv) *Organiser/Liaison Officer:* with the Director, to implement projects and programmes, and to have special responsibility in the areas of contact and co-ordination. Based in Cape Town.

Mr Neville Curtis has accepted this appointment. A graduate of the University of the Witwatersrand, Mr Curtis was vice-president of that University's SRC before becoming President of NUSAS (the National Union of South African Students) in 1970-1971.

DOCUMENT 10

FIVE BIBLICAL PRINCIPLES

Spro-cas is sponsored by the South African Council of Churches and the Christian Institute of Southern Africa. It thus has links with both the institutional Church and Christian bodies working in specialised fields. The work of Spro-cas is itself specialised and limited. It does not attempt to do the work of the Church, but to assist the Church in a specific way. It seeks some vision of what South African society could be if Christianity was taken seriously, and in what way churches, organisations, institutions, government departments and individuals can work towards such a society.

The following five Biblical Principles underlie the work of Spro-cas.

The Principle of Change

II Corinthians 5:17   There is a new world; the old order has gone, and a new order has already begun.

Galatians 6:16 Circumcision is nothing; uncircumcision is nothing; the only thing that counts is new creation! Whoever they are who take this principle for their guide, peace and mercy be upon them.

Revelation 21:5   Then he who sat on the throne said, Behold! I am making all things new.

Concepts like 'a new order', 'new creation', 'all things made new', are basic in the Biblical Message. The good news is the call to change from evil to good, and the possibility of this change taking place. In the Bible both man and society are seen to be in need of redemption. Our society too needs continual renewal. Christians should not fear such renewal or change, but welcome it, and see themselves as active collaborators in change. This is the call that comes to us through the Bible.

The Principle of Concern for Life

> Matthew 11:4-6   Go and tell John what you hear and see: the blind recover their sight, the lame walk, the lepers are made clean, the deaf hear, the dead are raised to life, the poor are hearing the good news.

> Matthew 25:36   For when I was hungry, you gave me food; when thirsty, you gave me drink; when I was a stranger you took me into your home; when naked you clothed me; when I was ill, you came to my help; when in prison you visited me.

> Matthew 15:32   I feel sorry for all these people; they have been with me now for three days and have nothing to eat.

When reading the Gospel narrative one clearly sees the deep concern Jesus had for life on all levels. Jesus is concerned about people who suffer from physical disability (sickness, cripples), economic deprivation (the poor), restrictions on their freedom (those in prison), alienation from society (lepers, mentally disturbed and prostitutes). While the Gospels focus on the situation of the individual and how his plight can be relieved, sociology, economics and political science today give us insight into the forces that shape our society. It would be plainly irresponsible today if we still confined our concern to providing relief for the individual, rather than changing those forces in society which cause deprivation and suffering.

The Principle of Christian Participation

> Luke 10:1   After this the Lord appointed a further 72 and sent them on ahead in pairs to every town and place he was going to visit himself.

> John 15:15   I call you servants no longer; a servant does not know what his master is about. I have called you friends, because I have disclosed to you everything that I heard from my father.

> Matthew 23:8   But you must not be called rabbi; for you have one Rabbi, and you are all brothers.

Jesus saw men as brothers, and as brothers they were called to share together in the Christian community. Man must not dominate nor exploit other men, politically, economically, spiritually or psychologically.

The Principle of Stewardship

Matthew 25:14 It is like a man going abroad, who called his servants and put his capital in their hands.

I Corinthians 4:2 Well then, stewards are expected to show themselves trustworthy.

I Peter 4:10 Whatever gift each of you may have received, use it in service to one another, like good stewards dispensing the grace of God in its varied forms.

Not only are we stewards of our own lives and abilities, but also of the land we live in, the soil, the water and the air. We are also stewards of the social processes under our control, whether it be as employer, committee member, or driver of a motorvehicle. It seems that westerners too often operate on a principle of ownership implying a responsibility only to self, whereas the Bible suggests rather a management principle where we are entrusted with resources and are responsible in using them to both God and our fellowmen.

The Principle of Human Worth

Luke 12:6 Are not sparrows five for twopence? And yet not one of them is overlooked by God. More than that, even the hairs of your head have all been counted. Have no fear; you are worth more than any number of sparrows.

Ephesians 2:10 For we are God's handiwork, created in Christ Jesus to devote ourselves to the good deeds for which God has designed us.

Galatians 3:28   There is no such thing as Jew and Greek, slave and free-man, male and female; for you are all one person in Christ Jesus.

Above all the Bible places a value on each person. Man has been re-evaluated in the death of Christ. The new man in Christ has been freed to devote himself to the renewal of the world. The freedom of the Christian is a freedom to be true man loved by Christ and free to love. Christian love overcomes the alienation between man and man. Christian love denounces as false all that humiliates man, all that restricts his freedom, all that oppresses him, all that exploits him and all that alienates him from his fellows.

Danie van Zyl
September, 1972

DOCUMENT 11

BLACK COMMUNITY PROGRAMMES
REPORT AND PROPOSALS

Introduction

The Black Community Programmes of Spro-cas 2 came into existence as a result of suggestions made by black staff appointed to join in the running of Spro-cas 2 programmes. Spro-cas 2 (Special Programme for Christian Action in Society) is a programme sponsored by the South African Council of Churches and the Christian Institute. The project was set up by the Churches 'to make a positive contribution to the creation of a better social order in South Africa, one based on Christian values such as justice, freedom and equality of opportunity'. The programme as designed by the Churches was meant to last for an initial period of two years, being reviewed in mid 1973. In a sense, the staff appointed to man the programme were given a 'blank cheque' to implement the broad goals in whatever way they saw fit.

With this in mind and also guided by an understanding of the complexity of the South African society, the staff of Spro-cas has adopted the approach of a dual thrust, with black staff planning programmes for the black community and white staff for the white community. It was from plans by the black staff that the Black Community Programmes were designed.

Rationale and Aims

The goals of the Black Community Programmes are:-

— to help the Black Community become aware of its own identity
— to help the Black Community to create a sense of its own power
— to enable the Black Community to organise itself, to analyse its own needs and problems and to mobilise its resources to meet its needs
— to develop Black leadership capable of guiding the development of the Black Community.

The underlying rati nale on which the B.C.P. bases its approach is that in South Africa part of the problem is the extent to which blacks have been made to depend upon white energy, leadership, guidance and trusteeship for most things relating to the direction of social change. Because of this, blacks have tended to voluntarily take a back seat in areas that were extremely crucial to their interests and have allowed themselves to develop feelings of inadequacy and inferiority. This therefore makes it necessary for relevant black work to direct itself amongst other things at eradicating the psychological oppression of blacks by their own over-sized mental image of the white man and his abilities and by their exaggerated feeling of powerlessness which results in lack of creative initiatives. Added to this, of course, is the desperate lack of skill arising out of a deliberate inadequacy of opportunities that characterises black life under white rule in South Africa.

Faced with these analyses, therefore, the B.C.P. have designed programmes in an attempt to contribute maximally to the direction of social change in South Africa.

Programmes

The areas of immediate concern in the B.C.P. have been religion, education, youth, welfare, culture, art.

Before going into detailed discussion of each field and related projects we need to point out that the B.C.P. adopts one or some of the following approaches to all the projects.

Initiating: In areas where a definite need exists but no agency or organisation is taking care of the need, we call together people interested in the need and capable of providing for it. Following an analysis of the extent and scope of the need and an examination of possible approaches towards provision for it, we make it possible for the setting up of an agency, organisation or functional structure that the participants may deem suitable as an answer to the needs.

Promotion: Where a need exists and some agency/agencies exist capable of answering to the needs but not fulfilling the task because of inadequacy or of misdirection of efforts, we call the groups concerned to a training seminar where the extent, and scope of the need is examined and the group's task and ability to serve the need are also examined. Ways and means of overcoming the hurdles are discussed and usually a positive approach is worked out.

Co-ordination: Where several agencies exist presumably serving the same interest but having no communication with each other, we create an opportunity for the groups concerned to come together to discuss their common goals, to work out ways and means of co-operation and where necessary to summate their strengths and resources for maximum efforts.

Enablement: This refers mainly to acquisition of skills by persons in leadership and functional positions within organisations. Shortage of skilled personnel in voluntary organisations is a plague common to most black organisations in South Africa. By making it possible for unskilled staff to acquire basic skills relating to their work, we play an 'enabling' role. In this regard we have and are compiling a list of trained people in the various areas of interest to black people. These people are from time to time required to offer their services in the training of voluntary workers.

Communication: Because of the absence of black-controlled press in the country, black people are often ignorant of what is going on in their ranks throughout the country. One of our tasks is therefore to conduct a survey of existing organisations in the black ranks and to be in constant contact with them, their frustrations and their achievements, and to inform the rest of the black world about these. This helps also in evoking spontaneous co-ordination plans amongst some organisations that suddenly discover their common goals and functions.

The actual projects that the B.C.P. has started working on or towards are:-

1   The Church Leaders' Project

In the first semester of 1972, a conference of Church leaders was convened to:

'bring together black Church leaders working in the so-called multiracial churches in South Africa with the view to examining their role within these churches and ways and means of increasing the effectiveness of their leadership for black people in black communities.'

Underlying this broad intention was the need to gain control over these churches whose membership is mostly black and to use the acquired power towards orientating church direction towards needs of the black people. Other short-term goals were looked at and ironed out in greater detail at a subsequent conference.

Briefly, the agreed goals of this project are:

(a)   to arrive at proper and well co-ordinated caucusing at local, regional and national denominational church conferences so that blacks can reflect their aims and goals in the general leadership of the various churches. To this end the B.C.P. are in constant communication with key people assigned to set up the machinery for these caucuses.

The testing grounds for the various caucuses are the regional and national meetings of these churches held in the latter half of 1972. Positive results have already been reported in some churches and further gains are expected to come from the national conferences.

(b)   to form non-denominational caucuses in various regions for the purposes of implementing the immediate goals such as:

Literacy campaigns: in South Africa there is an appallingly high rate of illitercay amongst the blacks. The Churches are the key people in the field of literacy because they are the only institutions allowed to run literacy schools besides government-approved agencies.

Social services bureau: this project is designed to cater for black people who suffer from social ills arising out of migratory labour, unemployment etc. It is meant to be a social advice bureau staffed by a number of experts equipped to deal with complex social problems. It will start on a voluntary basis but will ultimately work with a permanent staff.

The B.C.P. has been mandated to set up the caucuses that will work for these goals and to make sure that the programmes start by the beginning of January, 1973. In the field of literacy, liaison is to be established with groups like SASO. The B.C.P. Field Officers are currently undergoing training in literacy to facilitate training of literacy teachers.

(c) to work for the spread of Black Theology through the setting up of discussion groups and seminars on the topic. The B.C.P. are part sponsors towards the establishment of a Black Theology Agency that will control the content, nature, study and dissemination of all information and literature on Black Theology in South Africa. The agency will also compile courses on Black Theology for incorporation into study courses at the Theological Seminaries. A conference to launch this agency has been called for mid-February 1973 and one of the Field Workers of the B.C.P. is going on a tour of the country to canvass for this Agency among the religious groups operating in the black community.

(d) to influence black religious groups in the country towards adopting programmes in keeping with the aspirations of black people. Staff people do this by attending conferences of these religious groups to make well-considered and valuable suggestions for incorporation into the programmes of these organisations. Most of these efforts have been directed at the Interdenominational African Ministers' Association of Southern Africa (IDAMASA) and the African Independent Churches Association (AICA).

2   Youth Project

The B.C.P. has been the first organisation in the country to recognise the need for extensive organisation in the area of black youth. Prior to our efforts, most youth work, with the brilliant exception of the South African Students'

Organisation (SASO), has been completely irrelevant. In major big cities two types of youth organisations were prevalent — either the socially inclined type that concentrates on indoor games, picnics, dances etc. or the church oriented youth club that focuses attention on non-directional Bible Study classes, Sunday schools and other irrelevant though 'pious' pursuits.

The youth project consists in inviting these youth groups, together with other non-aligned youth individuals, to examine what real role they can play in the search for a proper identity by black people and to find out what their contribution can be in the total efforts by black people towards liberation.

To-date the B.C.P. have managed to set in gear a well directed drive by black youth in one province towards establishing a proper direction in their work. The Natal Youth Organisation is a result of an intensive training seminar that involved 10 youth groups from the Natal area. The organisation, which is still very young, is currently building up an extensive programme of self-help projects like literacy classes, establishment of clinics and other conscientisation programmes involving the proper interpretation of the worth and dignity of the Black man and his role in nation-building.

Similar training seminars have been planned for the other areas of the country. In October the Transvaal and Transkei will have their turn and in November and December, the Border, Eastern Cape and Western Cape areas will receive attention.

It is the goal of the B.C.P. to then call a national conference of all these regions in February/March 1973 towards the establishment of a National youth movement which will carry on the work that is currently being built up within youth ranks. The general intention of the project is to:-

(i)   make the youth attain a unanimity of purpose
(ii) sensitise the youth to social problems and the need for them to gear themselves towards social service
(iii) equip them with skills to function with maximum advantage
(iv) find means of finance for their initial launching.

3. Workers' Project

The African worker in South Africa is legally debarred from belonging to any recognised trade union. The current practice by employers is to set up Works Committees that are supposed to represent the interests of workers in each factory. These are very ineffective mouthpieces because of the total control that employers have over them.

On a national scale, the government policy is that 'Bantu' workers can be represented adequately through government instituted boards like the Wage Board which are then supposed to speak on behalf of the 'Bantu'.

For a long time people have been in constant search for a means of harnessing workers together for more effective bargaining. Being mostly unskilled, African workers are hired and fired at the will of employers who have adequate legal backing for their actions. Often employers go beyond their bounds but the workers are unable to respond in a meaningful way since they do not completely know their rights any more and in any case are aware that the system is geared to support the employer in any confrontation.

With this in mind, the B.C.P. working together with SASO have undertaken to sponsor a project that is geared at establishing a Black Workers' Council to look after interests of workers and to provide such benefits as are possible.

The Black Workers' Project is in 4 main phases:

a complete research into the various categories of industry and commerce that employ black workers. This will concentrate on legislation governing these categories and the kind of benefits and rights workers are entitled to versus those they actually get.

a tour of the country (which is divided into 5 regions) to identify and establish contacts with workers in the various areas; to acquaint the contacts with aims of the project and to train them in basic trade unionist principles so that they can act as local organisers.

a period during which to run regional seminars in the 5 regions in which the whole proposed scheme will be discussed.

a preparation of plans for the conference at which the actual Black Workers' Council will be discussed and adopted.

The 1st phase will also lead to the production of basic material on rights of workers, trade unionism etc.

The project is intended to round up in June 1973 with the calling of the Conference. The Black Workers' Council will be run within and across industry categories. Here the basic logic is that black workers have a lot of common interests that go beyond the factory where they work. They stay together in squalid conditions; they travel together in overcrowded trains and buses and in any case they are hired and fired at random and have to constantly sell their labour for a mere pittance.

The Black Community Programmes have seconded a staff man to this project. Full proposals relating to the project are separately available on request.

4   Culture/Welfare Project

This project started off with a survey of all cultural organisations that are run by black people for the black community. This covered both local and national organisations. This survey is still in progress.

The basic intention here is to make the B.C.P. a central registry of all community organisations with all the relevant data and information relating to each organisation. Following this three main things are intended to happen:-

(a)   a publication of a document listing all existing organisations and giving the necessary information and data relating to each. Important information here would be their addresses, aims, functional pattern, affiliations, financial position, publications etc.

(b)   a conference of groups that can be amalgamated for better function will then be called to accommodate this where possible.

(c)   skills training in community work will be conducted for the leadership of these organisations.

The publication referred to is scheduled to come out in December and whatever conference/conferences are required will then follow in the new year. Part of the aim here is to eradicate duplication where it exists and to improve on the efficiency of the leadership.

Arrangements have already been made for Consultation Seminars of all women groups in the country. These will be conducted on a regional basis, starting as from December to February. Similar conferences will be called for groups that can be grouped together.

5   Resource Centres

In an effort to promote black creativity, self-reliance and a sense of purpose, the B.C.P. are initiating as from the beginning of the new year the idea of Black Resource Centres to cater for the following needs:

(1)   to be centres where all information regarding statistics on black life can be found and used by black people.

(2)   to collect, display and sell black cultural artefacts in the fields of bead work, wood work, painting, art, sculpture etc.

(3)   to collect and maintain a library of speeches, talks, papers etc. delivered by black people on relevant topics. This is to be in tape and written form.

(4)   to collect and maintain a library of black poetry, music etc.

(5)   to collect for general readership all publications by black people in the country and abroad.

These will be day centres where people can come and read, refer, borrow, list material they need concerning black people.

It is intended that 3 such centres will be initiated in Durban, Johannesburg and Cape Town initially with intention to do the same in other areas of the country later on.

Suitably qualified people will be sought to maintain these centres.

6   Publications

The B.C.P. have three main publications:

(a)   a publication containing factual information on black organisations and their work. This has already been referred to above. It comes out once a year and merely has to be updated each year.

(b)   'Black Viewpoint': a quarterly publication on current topics in the country. This is intended to be a reflection of black thinking on matters of topical interests. In it we publish addresses given by black people on common topics.

(c)   'Black Review': This is a Year Book of activity by and against the black community. This will cover
        latest legislation affecting blacks
        political action by blacks
        political trends of thought in black circles
        major trials of black people
        activities in 'homeland' governments
        activities in sports bodies. etc.

It is mainly meant to be a reflection of whatever political activity and developments have taken place in a given year. This publication is preceded by intensive research into the fields it covers.

7. Implication of Projects

The implication of the projects outlined here are many. Amongst others are:

that the B.C.P. are faced with the problem of having to maintain for an initial period all the permanent structures/organisations or functional wings that come as a result of their efforts.
This therefore means that a floating fund to meet these needs if only partially, has to be established.

the projects mentioned here have to be looked at in conjunction with the existence of B.C.P. itself. The B.C.P. is not an organisation with an established membership. It is a completely sponsored project and hence has no funds beyond the grant from sponsors. We have already out grown the small sponsorship from the Council of Churches and Christian Institute by R10 000 for the year 1972 and will do so by much more next year.

the original 2 year programme drawn up by the sponsors was extremely unrealistic for the type of work we are now doing and hence alternative sources of sponsorship should be obtained for the envisaged expansion of work and for possible continuation of the project beyond 1973.

the B.C.P. have by their very nature to derive their authority from black people themselves and hence a complete break with the rest of the Spro-cas programme is in the logic of our development. It is our intention to call an evaluation conference of all the work we are doing in the black community in late June. At that point we expect all authority for the programmes to be taken up by the black community and a 'growing out' of our ties with the rest of the Spro-cas programme is a probable outcome.

inevitably the staff of the B.C.P. will have to grow in order to meet the demands of the work we are engaged in.

Staff and Offices

The Head office of the B.C.P. is at 86 Beatrice Street, Durban. This is where the Director of the programme operates from. In addition to the Head office two other regional offices have been opened — one in Durban and another in Johannesburg. The Durban regional office is attached to the Head office. A third regional office is scheduled to start operating in Cape Town as from the beginning of January 1973.

At present the B.C.P. has a staff of 3 — a Director and 2 Programme/Research Field workers. From the onset it has been the practice to attract onto the staff, people of varied experience in the fields to be covered by the programme.

Mr Bennie A. Khoapa an experienced social worker and a man of considerable experience in community development schemes is the Director of the programmes.

Mr Steve Biko an ex-student leader and founder president of the South African Students' Organisation (SASO). He has experience in the field of youth work and leadership training. Mr Biko is a Programme/Research Field Worker.

Mr Bokwe Mafuna an ex-journalist and experienced trade-unionist. As a journalist he worked primarily with black organisations and hence gained very basic understanding of the totality of black efforts and developed extensive contacts. Mr Mafuna is a Programme/Research Field Worker.

The two field officers are on national staff but are attached for convenience to offices at different regions. Mr Mafuna is attached to the Johannesburg office and Mr Biko to the Durban office. A third appointment is currently being considered for the Cape Town office if funds permit it.

Conclusion

We hope that this document will serve the purpose of providing as much information about the sum total of our projects as possible. Should there be any need for elaboration on any points contained herein, the B.C.P. will only be too happy to elaborate where necessary.

The need for an organisation like the B.C.P. being a central registry for black work cannot be overstressed. Modesty aside, we wish to state that the role we are playing is much more likely to bring to focus relevant approaches to be adopted in the direction of social change than has been done to date by most organisations. In serving this need, therefore, we would like to feel that we shall never be harnessed into inactivity by lack of funds. It is for this reason that a concerted appeal is being made to you.

B.A. Khoapa
December, 1972

DOCUMENT 12

SPRO-CAS WHITE PROGRAMMES: SOME PRELIMINARY WORKING NOTES

Rationale

(i) In the first place there are basic Christian convictions or ethical principles which motivate us. In the light of these it seems right that we should work for change in the present South African situation, that we should oppose injustice and seek to spread the truth, and that we should strive for human liberation, to help people become free of the psychological, ideological and material fetters that prevent them from being fully human. The specifically Christian aspect of this is dealt with in Rev. Danie van Zyl's five biblical principles. (see also Chapter 2 on 'The Responsible Society', Spro-cas Economics Report).

(ii) We accept as right and creative the division of Spro-cas into white and black programmes, as reflecting the differing needs of the two communities at this time. One of our assumptions, however, is that white people will always remain in South Africa, and that the two groups will thus have to achieve a basis for co-existence, involving participation in both political and economic structures. Thus the present white power structure is very real and whether they are for or against the status quo, whites are relevant. The role of whites who are really opposed to the status quo seems to us to be potentially very important at present: they have access to the white power structure which is denied to blacks. The crucial question for whites opposed to the status quo is how effective they are in working for change.

(iii) We accept that fundamental change in South Africa — in the sense of a radical redistribution of power, land and wealth — will ultimately be initiated and brought about by blacks. Up to that point of major change the potential role of whites who are really committed to change is of crucial importance.

(iv) The immediate question for such whites is whether they seek to be reformist or radical. For decades liberal whites have sought to be rhetorical guru's, assuming that they can convert the white masses. In what way do we seek to be different: realising that we are limited by certain realities of the South African situation, we yet try to be radical, i.e. in the sense of going to the roots of the problem — power and wealth; we try to pose really radical alternatives (e.g. 'The Eye of the Needle', and the work which has flowed from this);

we attempt to act as catalysts in situations e.g. within the Church, within these educational institutions — where potential for change exists; we do not draw back from tactics of confrontation where these seem to be creative and necessary;
we experiment with new change models (e.g. white consciousness);
we attempt to come to terms with our whiteness and not to cry out our guilt and frustration through multi-racialism for its own sake;
we are prepared to accept that we may fail in all or some of these;
above all, we recognise the need to be clearer about the society we want:
we see that it is essentially socialist in nature, and this gives us a greater stake in working for change, i.e. it is in our own interests to do so.

These are some of the ways in which we try to avoid the faults of the liberal-reformist approach, which seems to us to have helped merely to entrench the status quo. At the same time we recognise the value of working for certain reforms within the present system (as, for example, contained in some of the recommendations of the Spro-cas Commission reports).

(v)   We see our task as primarily within the white community, to prepare it for fundamental change, and to bring about such meaningful reform as possible. We are committed to working for the liberation of white people as a part of the creation of a liberated society.

(vi)   We see our work as being at two levels:

(a)   people — individual and groups.
(b)   structures.

(a)   In terms of people, we see a need to communicate information as effectively as possible about the nature of our society, and the role of whites — even well-meaning ones — in perpetuating its injustices and un-freedoms;
to assist whites to respond creatively to black initiative and black consciousness;
to propagate the concepts of white consciousness and of human liberation in all its aspects;
to inculcate through this an understanding of the need for change;
to assist in the formulation of effective strategies for change;
to assist in the co-ordination and implementation of strategies for change.

(b)   In terms of structures, we see a need to work as effectively as possible to modify those structures to which we have access (in church, education and the economic system) in order to enable black advancement;

to promote the idea of alternative structures and to promote and co-ordinate as effectively as possible efforts for change from within existing structures.

Basic to these endeavours, we see a need to collect and provide resources for ourselves and for the other agencies engaged in working for social change. Spro-cas can offer not only resources of a material nature (publications, posters, study aids, films etc) a human nature (staff, skills etc), but in itself by providing a model — structure, flexibility, program-orientated etc is a significant resource.

(vii)   In very broad terms we can see the following stages emerging from the thinking outlined above, and from our activities to date:

1968:   Theological clarification (The Message)

1969-72:   Study, reflection and publication (Study Commissions)

1972-73:   White consciousness programmes
            Church strategy
            Education strategy
            Economic strategy
            Contact and Co-ordination

1973-74:   The conscious building of a movement for social change, based on the previous, and possibly institutionalised. The emergence of certain on-going features from Spro-cas — which itself must die at the end of 1973.

            At some stage thereafter possibly the emergence of a new political movement.

4   Programmes

(i)   Church Programme

The Spro-cas Church report has provided us with an analysis and a set of recommendations in terms of which action can be taken. It is quite apparent at this stage that the Black Community Programme is directing its attention partly to the church as are other black groups in challenging the so-called multi-racial churches.

We believe the Church to be a major institution that controls power in this country: next to the institutions that control Education, the Economy and the Political system. Of these the church is the one that is most likely to have the potential to change the needs and demands of a new society. It is the only institution, as we see it, that can itself become an agent for real change. It is also the institution where we have leverage. As whites we therefore believe that much effort and attention should be directed at the church in a long programme of making it responsive and relevant to change. In Latin America such a programme, conducted over many years, has proved that the church suddenly provides crucial leadership. People such as Dom Helder Camara and Fr Torres. We thus see our role here, to challenge the church hierarchy and laity and respond constantly to all its manipulative and rascist machinery.·

Crucial to such a programme is a continuous careful analysis of all avenues of power in the church. We need to look to all the places where decisions are being taken for or on behalf of others (also whites). We need to look at the way the church spends and invests its money. Its style of glamour and affluence is out of keeping with the needs of the country and we need to challenge this. The white powered hierarchy of the church is a priority on the agenda of our programme.

(ii) *Resource Centre and Experimenting with New Communications Media*

In a number of fields we are doing the spade work for this already. This programme is designed for whites who are fighting the racism in white society.

All agencies or groups committed to change in South Africa are in need of resources of a material nature as well as a human nature. We can provide and are providing already a model (or models) which constitute such a service. To be relevant we need to communicate by posters, casette tapes, slide/tape shows, music, drama and films, and effective printed material. Through this we reach new audiences. The artist is crucial to the success of all of these, but if we accept that our media in the past have been one of the grestest failings in reaching an audience then this is a vital area in which to operate. Examples of this type of work in the U.S.A. have proved successful and contact with some such agencies has already influenced our work.

The entire Spro-cas (white) printing programme can be seen as the corner stone for the Resource and Communications centre.

(iii) Labour Programme

The basic motivation that we have in this field is the realisation that organisation of black workers will come from blacks. Our primary task is to try to utilise the access we have to the white power structure.

Our efforts in this sphere are at present concerned with the establishment of a code of employment practices and on another level we have been concerned with freeing blue prints for projects and freeing information in economic and labour matters, from individuals and institutions who have only academic, but no action use for them. We want this to be available to whomever might require it. We have tried to stimulate ideas in fields such as the Labour Advice Bureau or information on buying co-operatives. It is crucial that such work, however, does not become another talk saloon and *doing* is the purpose of such endeavour. The survey and subsequent action into church schools originates from the Labour Programme.

(iv) White Consciousness Programme

White Consciousness is the underlying philosophy for the above-mentioned programmes, but we visualise it as a separate action project at the moment as the concept still needs to be advocated and in fact has very little support at the moment.

Our target group in this sphere is first and foremost the liberal, affluent establishment. We are concerned here with their hypocrisy and the built-in racism/exploitation which they inflict daily through their institutions. White youth play a special role in this programme as they see themselves increasingly also being oppressed and shaped for one type of scoiety only. Their rejection needs to be guided towards some new society which we would broadly see as being socialist in nature.

The prime concern is to make whites realise that through their racism they have not only put the black man into a sociological jail, but they have put themselves into a sociological jail. We now want to get out of these imposed jails. Whilst we are in our jails we can never hope to work for any future society. A Spro-cas publication, *White Liberation,* is directed at the whites who seek change.

In the Education field, we need to experiment with what kind of education we feel is best for ourselves, our children. Such a group has been functioning for some two months and concentrates on reading and discussing new methods in education.

October 1972

DOCUMENT 13

ECONOMIC CHANGE IN SOUTH AFRICA

The demands for change in South Africa's economic system will accelerate in 1973, and the inherent weaknesses in our industrial relations system will become increasingly apparent.

These predictions are made by the Spro-cas Labour Panel which is actively following-up the recommendations contained in *Power, Privilege and Poverty*, the report of the Spro-cas Economics Commission which appeared in June 1972. Several recent developments in the South African industrial relations system indicate the validity of many of the findings in this report.

1   The Social Responsibility of Employers

There appears to be an increasing awareness among leading businessmen that employers have a social responsibility towards those they employ. This includes but goes beyond merely paying a just wage.

Recently this point was made by Mr van der Horst, the managing director of the Old Mutual, and by speakers at the Business Outlook Conference of the National Development and Management Foundation.

The question that must be asked is: 'What criteria are to be used in assessing whether employers are exercising their social responsibility. It is obviously inadequate for them merely to donate to charitable causes or merely to support ventures like TEACH and LEARN, worthwhile though these are. The crucial issue is whether employers are prepared to give all workers some form of worker representation.

The Spro-cas Economics Report has formulated six general principles which go some way towards providing a basis for the Responsible Society. They include the following:

Development exists for man, not man for development:
an economy which employs a worker may not accept his labour while rejecting his humanity.

The goal is not simply economic growth:
the lion's share of South Africa's increased wealth has gone to only a small proportion of the population, whilst in some sectors of the economy (the gold mines, the white-owned farms, and the reserves) the majority have actually grown poorer over time.

There must be no poverty in the midst of plenty.

Power should be shared:
the dignity of every worker must be respected in that he should have a voice in the conduct of industry or business which is carried on by means of his labour.

Spro-cas is now attempting to formulate specific criteria for employment practices which can be presented for consideration by both employers and labour leaders in 1973.

2 Apprenticeship Training

The expulsion by the Motor Industry Employees' Association of some motor car mechanics for training Coloured apprentices highlights the conflict between white workers about the training of black apprentices.

It is significant that the Motor Industry Combined Workers' Union, the Coloured Union in the motor trade, has now demanded access to the relevant Apprenticeship Committees. The Spro-cas Economics Commission recommended in this regard:

'That the limitations imposed by apprenticeship committees on blacks being trained as apprentices be abolished, and that apprenticeship training for blacks be expanded'
(Recommendation 7).

This recommendation was forwarded to the Department of Labour and the Acting Secretary of Labour replied: 'I have to inform you that the Department is not prepared to enter into correspondence with the Commission on matters of Government policy'.

It is in the public's interest for Apprenticeship Committees to have to account for their activities. South Africa has the world's highest death rate as a result of motor car accidents, and steps should be taken to ensure that there are sufficient apprentices to service motor cars and trucks. With a shortage of 2 000 apprentices per year, it must be expected that there are cars on the road which have not been properly serviced. The public should demand that Apprenticeship Committees do not use arbitratory powers to prevent competent people from receiving training.

Appendix

3   Danger to the Continued Existence of the Industrial Councils

The Spro-cas Economics Commission expressed concern that Industrial Councils, which are important organisations in maintaining labour peace, face a crisis. It is significant that the Building Industry Federation of South Africa recently commented on the future of the Industrial Council for the Building Industry, whose continued existence is endangered by the decline in membership of registered trade unions. With the increased absorption of African workers, who may not belong to legally recognised unions, other industries will undoubtedly begin to face the same crisis.

The Spro-cas Economics Commission endorsed the right of all workers to belong to legally recognised trade unions. There is no hope of long-term industrial 'peace in South Africa unless this principle is accepted and implemented.

4   Worker Participation

One of the most explicit recommendations of the Spro-cas Economics Report deals with the establishment of Works Committees as a first step towards giving all workers the right to participate in the decision-making process regarding their wages and working conditions. This requirement is increasingly being mentioned by leading businessmen, but again no clear definition has emerged as to the actual step to be taken to achieve worker participation for all workers.

The Spro-cas recommendation is as follows:

'Works committees should be established in any undertaking employing 50 workers or more, the following conditions being borne in mind.

(a)   that a national body of works committees be established, in order that experience may be shared and direction given;

(b)   that works committees should have access to relevant Industrial Councils and the Wage Board;

(c)   that members elected to serve on works committees should be given specific training regarding their role as representatives of the workers.'

The Commission drew attention to the fact that, although provision for works committees is contained in legislation, very few such committees have been established — in less than a half per cent of all registered factories. Works committees can serve a useful purpose in creating recognised channels of communication and providing their members with experience in the process of negotiation.

Hopefully, 1973 will see a far more determined use of the system of works committees.

5 The PUTCO Strike and the Dockworkers' Strike

The outcome of the PUTCO strike has indicated the inevitability of having to accommodate workers' demands irrespective of whether they have legally recognised rights or not. The PUTCO drivers not only achieved a substantial increase in pay amounting to 33% but the charges against them of illegal strike action were dropped. The more recent dockworkers' strikes in Cape Town and Durban have also shown that the Government and employers have no alternative when workers take a stand but to accept that some drastic improvement has to be made and that some form of consultation with them has to be instituted.

Is it necessary for the economy to be disrupted by strike action? Cannot management in particular adopt a positive attitude towards industrial relations?

Conclusion

The report of the IMF delegation has highlighted again the need for both trade unions and employers in South Africa to take positive steps to meet the developing crisis in the industrial relations system.

There are immediate areas of injustice and inequality which call for urgent action. The stage has passed where statements about the problem will suffice. What are now required are specific programmes with pre-determined objectives (like just wages, worker representation, social security of workers and their families, productivity etc.) If this is not done by those who at present have the resources and facilities, then those who are at the moment unorganised will seek redress. The Spro-cas Labour Panel is working towards the formulation of specific recommendations for employment practices in line with the concept of the Responsible Society.

3 November, 1972

L.G.C. Douwes Dekker
Convenor, Spro-cas Labour Panel

Peter Randall
Director

DOCUMENT 14

SPRO-CAS: MOTIVATIONS AND ASSUMPTIONS

WE ARE a deeply divided society and the needs of the black community and those of the white community are very different. To attempt to meet those needs through a 'traditional' multi-racial strategy is likely to be unsuccessful — there is much evidence of this in our past history — and hence Spro-cas 2 is clearly demarcated into Black Community Programmes and White Consciousness Programmes, each with its own director and staff, the former based in Durban and the latter in Johannesburg. (Since a description of the Black Community Programmes should clearly only be provided by those engaged in them, I shall refer interested readers to the B.C.P. Director, Mr Bennie A. Khoapa).

Spro-cas 2 is the second phase of a project working for a more just social order in South Africa. The initials stand for Special Project for Christian Action in Society. Spro-cas 2 is a follow-up to the Study Project on Christianity in Apartheid Society (Spro-cas 1), which began in mid-1969. The entire project is due to finish at the end of 1973, although certain independent on-going activities may emerge from it.

Spro-cas is sponsored by the South African Council of Churches and the Christian Institute. It thus has links with both the institutional Church and Christian bodies working in specialised fields. The work of Spro-cas is itself specialised and limited. It does not attempt to do the work of the Church, but to assist the Church in a specific way. It seeks some vision of what South African society could be if Christianity were taken seriously, and in what way churches, organisations, institutions, government departments and individuals can work towards such a society.

The specifically Christian dimension underlying the work of Spro-cas has been spelt out by my colleague, the Rev. Danie van Zyl, who identifies five biblical principles:

> The principle of change and renewal
> the principle of concern for life
> the principle of Christian participation
> the principle of stewardship, and
> the principle of human worth.

The document in which Mr van Zyl deals with these principles is available on request from Spro-cas. Let me merely quote two brief extracts as illustrative of the ethical concerns which guide us:

> 'Not only are we stewards of our own lives and abilities, but also of the land we live in, the soil, the water, and the air. We are also stewards of the social processes under our control, whether it be as employer, committee member, or driver of a motor vehicle. It seems that westerners too often operate on a principle of ownership implying a responsibility only to self, whereas the bible suggests rather a management principle where we are entrusted with resources and are responsible in using them to both God and our fellowman ...'

And:

> 'The freedom of the Christian is a freedom to be true man loved by Christ and free to love.
> Christian love overcomes the alienation between man and man.
> Christian love denounces as false all that restricts his freedom, all that oppresses him, all that alienates him from his fellows'.

Besides these Christian principles, which allow us no option but to see ourselves as needing to be active collaborators in social change in our situation, we base our approach on a number of assumptions about the nature of our society and strategies for change. These can be only briefly outlined in this article.

One of our assumptions is that white people will always remain in South Africa, and that the groups will thus have to achieve a basis for co-existence, involving participation in political and economic structures. We believe that the search for an alternative society that will make this possible is only just beginning.

We accept that fundamental change in South Africa — in the sense of a radical redistribution of power, land and wealth — will ultimately be initiated and brought about by blacks. We thus believe that the Black Community Programmes are both potentially and actually the most important single aspect of Spro-cas, and the white staff have taken a deliberate decision to phase the white programmes out before the end of the project in favour of the black ones, if we are unable to meet our full budget requirements for the year. It is significant that the B.C.P.'s share of the total Spro-cas budget has increased from about 20 per cent to more than 50 per cent over the past year.

The crucial question for whites opposed to the status quo is how effective they are in working for change (much of our own thinking in this regard is shaped by the excellent chapters on Strategies for Change in *Towards Social Change,* the report of the Spro-cas Social Commission). The immediate question for white opponents of the status quo is whether they seek to be reformist or radical. For decades liberal whites have sought to exhort and convert the white masses. That this is largely a futile and even counter-productive exercise hardly needs stating. The Social Report clearly indicates the hopelessness of reacting to superficial events in our national life, which 'alternately ignite or extinguish sporadic flickers of hope for change'. This sensitivity to the superficial 'blinds many people to the lessons of past decades, during which the basic structure of inequality has persisted despite many marginal adjustments in political terminology and practice' *(Towards Social Change* p. 158).

The necessary starting point for work for change then is an understanding of the basic social forces in our country. The reports of the various Spro-cas study commissions and the publications of the Black Community Pro-grammes have helped us to understand just how profoundly entrenched in our social system are the basic patterns of inequality, injustice and dis-crimination which have endured despite 'marginal adjustments'. That they run right into all our social institutions, including the body of the church itself, is clearly revealed in the report of the Church Commissions, and in a subsequent survey which Spro-cas carried out into the wages and conditions of work of black employees in church schools (the average wage, for example, was R36 p.m. and one church school in the Transvaal worked its black employees for ten hours a day, seven days a week, and paid them an average of R18 p.m.).

It is necessary at the same time to recognise that we are all part and parcel of a system of exploitation, and if we are white we inevitably enjoy the benefits of this whether we consciously wish to or not. We are thus, in black eyes, part of the problem. It is our decision whether we wish rather to become part of the solution. Our understanding of the moral imperative sketched above seems to leave us with no option.

At the same time the system of exploitation (perhaps the most effective form of labour exploitation, more effective even than slavery, according to the Spro-cas Economics Commission) which provides us with material benefits, also damages us gravely, reducing our liberty and lessening our humanity. To recognise the harm being done to us, as whites, is probably a necessary starting point for effective work towards change. The concept of 'white con-sciousness', which embraces this, is explored in *White Liberation,* published by Spro-cas in February, and edited by my colleague, Horst Kleinschmidt.

Realising that we are necessarily limited by certain realities of the South African situation, including the draconian powers contained in legislation, we yet aim for a radical approach, i.e. in the sense of going to the roots of the problem — power and wealth. Merely to list the pre-conditions that the Economics Commission found to be necessary for fundamental change (radical redistribution of power, land and wealth referred to earlier) indicates both the extent of the task and the dimensions of the new society:

the right of all people to effective political power;
the right of all workers to belong to legally recognised trade unions;
a significant redistribution of land;
a significant redistribution of wealth and income;
radical changes to the existing educational system, and the right of all to equal access to education;
the right of all people to effective social security benefits.
(Power, Privilege and Poverty, p. 104).

Recognising that such fundamental change may not in fact be possible within the present political and economic structures, we seek to post really radical alternatives, and see the urgent need for a serious consideration of socialism and such concepts as participatory democracy and workers' control. (See, for example, *The Eye of the Needle* by Richard Turner, reviewed in the January issue of Reality).

The white staff of Spro-cas see our task as primarily within the white community, to prepare it for fundamental change, and to bring about such meaningful reform as possible (as, for example, contained in some of the recommendations of the six Spro-cas Commission reports). We are committed to working for the liberation of white people as a part of the creation of a liberated society. Part of this task is the need to communicate effectively with our own community, and we try to do this not only through our growing body of publications, which range from a scholarly study of *Migrant Labour* by Dr Francis Wilson to a collection of poems *(Cry Rage!)* by two black writers, and our posters, dossiers, study aids and the background papers, but also through small group workshops and seminars and public meetings (such as a series of lectures on 'The Need for Reform in South Africa', to be held in Johannesburg during February — March). We see the need to be experimental and flexible, and to risk the inevitable controversies.

We see, as part of this, a need to work as effectively as possible to modify those structures to which we have access (in church, education and the economic structure), and hence we have been pursuing programmes in these three areas and will continue to do so until Spro-cas ends. Workshops, seminars and public conferences form part of this, as do participation in the events of 'change' organisations, and the provision of resource material and personnel to assist such organisations. Another feature of this is our contact and co-ordination programme which seeks to assist 'change' organisations to plan effectively and to co-ordinate their efforts. We also provide consultancy services and are collecting relevant audio-visual and other resources.

I am very conscious that these notes are much more an attempt to sketch the rationale for Spro-cas than a detailed description of our work. But the work is meaningful only in the context of our motivation and our understanding of the situation, and those who are really interested can always enquire further. Spro-cas is a short-term project and not an organisation, and is thus constantly moving and changing to meet new issues and new situations. One of our freedoms is that we do not have a vested interest in self-perpetuation.

Peter Randall,
Reprinted from *Reality*,
March 1973.

DOCUMENT 15

A PROGRAMME FOR SOCIAL CHANGE

First, preliminary draft

A programme for social change can be seen as developing through several stages, not necessarily chronologically distinct, but tending to overlap and merge:

1 *A preparatory stage* in which awareness is developed of the need for fundamental change, hope is aroused of the possibility of change, and the realisation is created that individuals and groups can assist in bringing about change.

2 *An organizational stage* in which specific groups and organisations of different types are created: e.g. local action groups and committees, caucuses, supportive groups etc.

3 *Action stage* in which direct strategies are developed. At this stage there may be a coalescing of forces into a broad movement with defined social and political goals.

The first preparatory stage has been under way for some considerable time in South Africa. The churches, the English-language universities, the South African Institute of Race Relations, the Black Sash, the Christian Institute, the English press, NUSAS, other agencies, and Spro-cas itself, have all seen an important part of their function to warn whites of the need for change, to create awareness of the injustices in the system etc. There has been an understandable general reluctance to move beyond this stage of dissemination of information and exhortation for change. It is our intention to work with those who have gone beyond this and to assist others in becoming relevant as change agents by setting themselves 'doing' objectives.

Since whites as a group are the beneficiaries of the system, the preparatory stage has had limited success, and the mass of whites is probably far more concerned to prevent fundamental change than to enable it to occur. But there is a limited constituency of whites — in the churches, amongst academics and students, in the 'change' organisations, and some individuals scattered throughout the community — who are aware of the need for fundamental change and have some understanding of what this implies. We would, for example, see it as crucial to be able to discard strategies and operations that have become outdated (or fallacious).

To some extent the second, organisational, stage has been with us for some time. Various action-orientated groupings have emerged — e.g. Spro-cas 2, the Wages Commissions — but the present picture is of diffuse, unco-ordinated activity occuring rather haphazardly and sporadically.

So at present the need seems to be to concentrate on this stage, while further preparatory work in terms of the first stage continues, and becomes increasingly more sophisticated and effective in its techniques. The aim is to move as rapidly and coherently as possible into the third, coalescing, stage. From this stage may come a broadly based consensus amongst those whites working for change, in which there is agreement on the social, economic and political objectives for the society — thus providing the potential for a new political force.

A number of assumptions underlie our own approach:

1   We are increasingly entering a period of successive crises and confrontations (between black and white:labour/management; homeland leaders/central government; students/university authorities; black drama and poetry; within the 'multi-racial' churches; and also between younger and older whites over questions of authority and life-style etc, e.g. the Schlebusch Commission). This period will be aggravated by international tensions (foreign investment, South West Africa, liberation movements etc).

2   The short term response of the South African government is likely to be increasingly repressive and totalitarian, thus aggravating the potentials for conflict.

3   The need is for fundamental change in the sense of a radical redistribution of land, power and wealth (with the kind of pre-conditions listed in the Spro-cas Economics Report, p. 103-104).

4   Such fundamental change will be initiated by blacks, not whites. We are perhaps already entering a period of transition in which the initiative is passing into black hands (labour, Black Theology, Black Consciousness, Buthelezi, Matanzima, Phatudi etc).

5   Under these circumstances there are various implications for whites wishing to see fundamental change:

(i)   to stop acting as obstacles to black advancement (by wresting initiatives, by acting as spokesmen for blacks, by pursuing the multi-racial strategy which saps black solidarity, by perpetuating black dependency through paternalism and charity etc);

(ii) to work primarily within the white community, preparing it for change, modifying those structures which are amenable for change, mobilising forces for white liberation etc.

6 When fundamental change occurs it will be important that there should be a body of whites who have thought through and accepted its implications, who will be available for negotiation, and who will co-operate with and support black leadership by providing some of the necessary skills and resources.

In summary, we see the need for the conscious development of a programme for fundamental change amongst whites, to operate parallel to initiatives that are developing in the black community, and to be guided by the above considerations.

We envisage the following features for such a programme:

1 It should have a clearly identifiable title.
2 It should seek to identify those individuals and groupings who are actually or potentially working for fundamental change. The specifics of fundamental change will have to be spelt out in detail by those who see themselves as part of such a programme.
3 It should bring them into meaningful contact with each other, through meetings, conferences, newsletters and a magazine to support the political thrust which could emerge, etc.
4 It should seek to establish a common pool of resources (human skills, organisational abilities, physical resources like literature, films, multi-media creations etc) on which such people can draw.
5 Organisationally, the simplest way to do this would seem to be through affiliation of individuals and groups to the programme at reasonable fees which would help to meet the costs involved.
6 The affiliates could elect a co-ordinating body which would meet from time to time as necessary.
7 The day-to-day work to be carried out by a small, versatile secretariat, highly mobile and flexible in nature.
8 The main functions of the programme could be summarised as follows:

(i)   Contact and sharing of information, plans and skills amongst those who imaginatively and creatively work towards their objectives.
(ii)   Co-ordinating of activities where necessary and desirable.
(iii) Sharing and pooling of resources.
(iv)   Clarifying of objectives and strategies.
(v)   Identifying areas of action and assisting in the development of programmes and projects to fit these.
(vi)   Longer-range planning (into Stage 3).

In general, the programme would provide a supportive, co-ordinating framework for those whites working for change. It would not seek to establish ideological consensus nor even general agreement on strategy, since these exercises at the present time are likely to result in unproductive debate only. It would be responsive to the needs of those in particular situations who need information, assistance, resources, support and guidance on strategy. In its own strategy it should confront rather than compromise. It would not seek to lay down policy directives for those in the field or to impose patterns of activity.

It would not be elitist and bureaucratic, but grass-roots and non-authoritarian, with a modest budget and life-style. It would not seek to draw members from existing agencies, but to support those members where relevant. It should be experimental, in the sense that the co-ordinating group would regularly review its rationale and functions and be prepared, if necessary, to make radical changes, or even to disband the programme.

Much of this proposal is based on our own experience in Spro-cas 2, where we have increasingly been called on to perform the functions listed above, and have become increasingly aware that no agency at present exists which can effectively fulfill them. The staff of Spro-cas have no stake in extending the life of the Spro-cas project itself however. Part of the value in Spro-cas is that it has functioned as a short term project and it should not become institutionalised. In addition, the Spro-cas framework may not be wide enough to cater for or encompass all those groups who might want to be involved in the proposed programme. Individuals with skills (architects, businessmen, artists and poets) and groups (like the Justice and Peace groupings in the Roman Catholic Church, groups of students etc) have called on us to help them meet their needs for meaningful action for change. They need the sort of supportive, co-ordinating framework we propose.

During April, Spro-cas staff have consulted with people in Johannesburg, Pretoria, Durban Pietermaritzburg, East London, Alice, Kingwilliamstown, Grahamstown, Port Elizabeth, Stellenbosch and Cape Town. In meetings with over a hundred whites we have received general encouragement for the thinking outlined in this memorandum. They include church leaders, academics, trade union leaders, students and writers and journalists.

Spro-cas can play an enabling role in the setting up of the programme, providing staff, resources and administrative services until the end of 1973, when Spro-cas comes to an end. By then, hopefully, the programme will have acquired a momentum of its own.

The programme can be seen as an organic development out of Spro-cas, and would gain from the existence of two other major Spro-cas outgrowths, the Black Community Programmes and the establishment of a publishing and communications centre.

10/5/1973

DOCUMENT 16

SPRO-CAS POLITICAL REPORT: PRESS RELEASE

1 Background

Since 1969 the members of the Spro-cas Political Commission have been investigating the political system in South Africa and grappling with the problem of political change in this country.

Their final report, *South Africa's Political Alternatives*, is now ready and will be publicly released on *8 June 1973*. Advance copies have been sent to the Prime Minister, the leaders of the White Opposition parties, the Coloured political parties, the S.A. Indian Council and the leaders of the homelands governments.

Thirteen members of the Commission have signed the Report. They include Prof. Tony Mathews (the chairman), Mr Leo Marquard, Dr Beyers Naudé, Mr André du Toit, Dr David Welsh, Mr René de Villiers and Dr Oscar Wollheim. Minority reports by Dr Edgar Brookes and Dr Denis Worrall are included in the report. The names of Mr Japie Basson M.P. and Dr G.F. Jacobs M.P. appear as consultants.

Two members of the Commission died before the report was finalised. They were Dr W.F. Nkomo and Prof. Donald Molteno. Two other members were banned by the South African government. They are Dr Rick Turner and Mr Justice Moloto.

South Africa's Political Alternatives is the last report to be issued by the six Spro-cas study commissions. The study project was established in 1969 under the sponsorship of the S.A. Council of Churches and the Christian Institute of Southern Africa.

Since the beginning of 1972, the Special Programme for Christian Action (Spro-cas 2) has been acting as a follow-up project to the work of the Commissions. Dr Worrall gives the 'activistic' role of Spro-cas 2 as his reason for not signing the Political Report.

More than 20 000 copies of the previous five Spro-cas commission reports have been distributed. They are: *Education beyond Apartheid* (1971), *Towards Social Change* (1971), *Power, Privilege & Poverty* (1972), *Apartheid and the Church* (1972) and *Law, Justice and Society* (1972). Altogether, more than 150 South Africans have participated in the work of the six Spro-cas commissions.

Besides the six commission reports, Spro-cas has published more than a dozen other publications since its inception, in addition to background papers, study aids, posters, dossiers and photographic displays. The final report arising from the study project (Spro-cas 1) will be a co-ordinated report, which is expected later this year.

The whole Spro-cas project will be completed at the end of 1973, when Spro-cas will go out of existence. Plans are now being formulated for a number of projects to come out of the work and experience of Spro-cas.

2 Political Report

The preface to the Report says that 'it offers a realistic and constructive way through the darkness that seems to lie ahead'. The Report starts by enunciating the ethical principles that should underlie the political system and warns that any political formula or system which does not embody these ethical principles stands no real chance of success.

From such primary ethical principles as equality, freedom, justice and responsibility, the Commission derives concepts such as the Rule of Law, Guaranteed Civil Rights and Effective Participation in Government. These concepts are analysed at some length to provide an ethical framework for the remainder of the Report.

Present Political Position

Against the background of this ethical framework, the Commission analyses the present political position in South Africa, finding it 'a racial oligarchy in which all significant political power is vested in white hands'. It traces the steady erosion of black rights and the growth of white power and privilege, pointing out that the ethical principles enunciated earlier have been consistently violated.

One of the major conclusions in this section of the Report is that 'order of a kind and of a questionable permanence has indeed maintained in our society, but it has extracted a high toll in terms of freedom. Over wide areas civil liberties have been eclipsed and the Rule of Law put in abeyance. The Security Police and the Bureau for State Security operate with what appears to outsiders as an infinite scope. Informers are believed to be at work in every corner of society; it is widely believed that telephones are tapped and that mail is interfered with. All these activities create a widespread fear in our society that these security agencies are steadily becoming a law unto themselves'.

The Commission finds that the real issue is not the supposed antithesis between order and freedom: 'it is the real conflict between supporting the existing social structure and ideas and actions that strive to change it.' The real aim of much security legislation and action is 'to shore up the existing unequal order and to frustrate the evolution of a more just order'.

The Commission believes that 'the rhetoric and the actions aimed at the goal of self-preservation are having catastrophic effects on white society', breeding values 'that are the antithesis of love, compassion and humanity'. It warns 'in the strongest terms that the growth of a militarist spirit is a serious cancer which, if unchecked, will nullify any claims which white South Africans may have to being custodians of the Judaeo - Christian tradition'.

The Commission then analyses the political dimensions of the policy of separate development, finding that it is completely inadequate as a means of ensuring the ethical principles previously enunciated, providing, for example, little hope of equality and of effective participation in government by all people.

In considering the possible forces for change in the present political position, the Commission sees little likelihood of revolution in the near future. After considering the impact of black consciousness, including labour unrest, economic forces and foreign pressures, the Commission emphasises that 'unless structural changes are made in the political system there are grave dangers facing South Africa: it may degenerate into a 'garrison-state', a type of totalitarian society in which all the liberties of all the citizens are stifled; or there may be violence'.

'There is', the Commission concludes, 'a long-run danger that the entire sub-continent may become engulfed in a race war whose possibilities of escalation are incalculable'.

Proposals for Change

Accepting the urgent need for major change in the political system, the Commission recognises that this will require sacrifice, courage and the casting out of fear, since white South Africans 'can achieve security only by admitting their black fellow-citizens to an effective share of political participation and by collaborating with them in building an open society whose foundations are justice, liberty and mutual esteem'.

'The challenge is a great one: the major problem of our times is the world-wide inequality of black and white. South Africa is a microcosm of this world, and if South Africans can rise to the challenge their contribution will not only have been to their country but also to mankind.'

To assist in meeting this challenge, the Commission offers a set of detailed proposals in the form of a 'model for transition' from the present apartheid system in the direction of a more open and equal society.

This model is the culmination of the report and repays careful study. It is divided into two stages:

(a)   the first stage aims at the greatest measure of non-discrimination and
      equality possible in the present society and a progressive pluralistic
      devolution of power starting from the present political system.

(b)   the second stage suggests the main outlines of a more open pluralistic
      society and the basic structure of a new political system embodying a
      federal multi-racial government.

Throughout, the Commission tests its proposals against two basic questions: What is ethically acceptable? What is practically feasible? It is the proposals in the 'model of transition' that offer the 'realistic and constructive
way through the darkness that seems to lie ahead'.

(Note: Reviewers may wish to begin with the recommendations and conclusions contained in chapters twelve and thirteen, and then refer back to the
body of the report for substantiating data and the reasoning behind the proposals).

Significance of the Report

A number of points should be stressed about the Report as a whole and the
Model for Transition in particular:

1   The Report is *not* simply another abstract and polemical exercise along
the familiar lines of the liberal - progressive tradition in South Africa.
Though there is a clear continuity with the fundamental moral and political
principles of that tradition, the Report is primarily characterised by the
attempt to apply these principles realistically in the pluralistic situation of
South Africa, and as such it constitutes an important new departure.

2   The Report offers a *comprehensive* framework for, and analysis of,
political change in South Africa. There have been various proposals in recent
years, including the other Spro-cas reports, but they have not previously been
integrated into a systematic discussion of the major problems and alternatives.

3   It must be stressed that this comprehensive model is essentially a *multiple
strategy* for change, taking into account the various factors in the political
system and the various possibilities of change.

4   The emphasis in Part Four of the Report on *pluralistic* thinking in politics
should not on any account be construed as implicit support for Separate
Development. The Report unambiguously rejects both the present practice of
apartheid (in Part Two) and the theoretical goals and principles of the policy
as well (in chapter 8).

5   The Report should therefore be clearly differentiated from the efforts of those 'idealistic' critics of the present implementation of the policy who favour a more 'consistent' or 'radical' implementation of Separate Development. In so far as the Report 'accepts' some of the institutions created in terms of the present policy, this does *not* mean any support for the government's scheme for the homelands. On the contrary, the Report comes out unambiguously against the option of 'independence' for the homelands, and sees the significance of these institutions in terms only of a possible framework for bargaining and consultation with the central (white) government.
6   The Report is also marked by a thorough criticism of the traditional liberal-constitutional approach and of the Westminister-type democratic model in South African conditions (Chapter 9). Moreover, it attempts to develop a general theoretical framework for the analysis of political conflict in plural societies (Chapter 10).

One of the themes of the Spro-cas Political Report is that change is inevitable. Our society is volatile and dynamic, and 'the proclaimed intentions of governments are seldom realised in ways that their leaders might anticipate or desire'.

Ascension Day
Republic Day, 31 May, 1973.

Peter Randall
Director, Spro-cas

DOCUMENT 17

August 3, 1973.

Sir de Villiers Graaff M.P.
Cape Town.

AN OPEN LETTER TO THE LEADER
OF THE OPPOSITION

Dear Sir de Villiers,

I understand that two attempts have been made to serve a subpoena on me to appear before the Schlebusch Commission. A subpoena has already been served on another member of my staff, Mrs Ilona Kleinschmidt. This is presumably in connection with the investigation into the South African Institute of Race Relations; if so, this is clearly absurd in the case of Mrs Kleinschmidt, who has no connections with that Institute whatsoever.

However, that is not my main reason for writing. I address myself to you as Leader of the Official Opposition to make it clear that I and other members of Spro-cas staff are not under any circumstances prepared to testify before the Commission, and that we are fully prepared for any consequences that this may bring for us.

We have always done our work in the open and have never concealed any of our activities, and would be very willing to appear before an impartial judicial commission should an enquiry be considered necessary. I have stated this previously and was a co-signatory to a statement to this effect issued recently which was also signed by the Chairman and Director of the Christian Institute, the Cape Regional Director of the Christian Institute, the editor of *Pro Veritate,* and the General Secretary of the South African Council of Churches. I mention this to make it clear that refusal to testify before the Schlebusch Commission in no way indicates that I have anything to hide.

My reasons for refusing to co-operate with that Commission are as follows:

1. The decision of the two major white parties to collaborate on such a commission must be seen in the context of the utterly dangerous situation developing in our country between the forces of change and the forces of reaction. As the pressures of change increase, the great danger is that the

white political parties will move closer together in order to suppress them, and we are clearly in a period where dissent and protest are being met with increasing intolerance. Our immediate future is likely to be marked by a more rapid movement towards totalitarianism. This can only increase the polarisation already occurring and ultimately set the stage for a massive and uncontrollable confrontation, which, as a South African, I wish to do anything possible to avoid.

2.   The collaboration of your party with the government in the Schlebusch Commission seems to me to be symbolic of the dangerous drift towards a basic 'consensus' on 'law and order' in the face of pressures for change. In the process, justice suffers, and men of conscience must inevitably find themselves in a difficult position.

3.   Parliament developed to counter the tyranny of rulers who had un-fettered powers to take arbitrary actions against individuals. The parliamentary system has been the result of a long battle to secure the freedom of individual citizens from arbitrary restrictions by the state. One of the most vital elements of this system is the separation of the legislature and the judiciary.

4.   In South Africa we now have the danger of parliament itself acting in a tyrannical way in that both parties are collaborating in a process which:

(a)   by-passes the judiciary and removes from individuals the protection of the courts;

(b)   results in individual citizens who have not had the right of a fair trial and against whom no charges have been proven being subjected to the most grievous loss of personal liberty.

5.   Parliament, by agreement of both governing and opposition parties, has set up a commission of enquiry, composed of its own members, who, by your own admission, cannot be fair and impartial judges in a matter such as this. This commission operates in secret and people appearing before it are denied the most elementary rights of justice: they do not know what charges they are accused of, they may not cross examine any witnesses who may testify against them, they are not allowed adequate legal representation, they do not have access to secret information from unnamed sources etc, etc., they may then receive severe punishment

from the government and have no recourse to the courts. In the case of 8 NUSAS leaders this involved banning; in the case of Wilgespruit staff this involved a public smear of grotesque proportions. Even the reasoned rebuttal by the joint commission of the South African Council of Churches and the Wilgespruit Management Committee, under the chairmanship of a distinguished former chief Justice of Botswana, of all the major allegations levelled against Wilgespruit by the Schlebusch Commission cannot fully offset the damage done to these people.

Under the circumstances it seems clear to me that to participate in any way in this process is to be party to a gross prostitution of democracy, and my conscience will not allow me to do so.

I believe that history will judge your party in the harshest terms if it continues to collaborate with the government in this commission. If I and others are to be punished for our refusal to co-operate with the commission we shall have to regard the United Party as party to a shameful act. I appeal to you in the name of justice and in the light of the desperate need to preserve those vestiges of the democratic process that remain in South Africa to withdraw your party from the Schlebusch Commission. I believe that this is a matter of urgent public concern, and so I feel it is necessary to make this letter public.

Yours sincerely,

Peter Randall
Director

INDEX